THANKS FOR
THE GAME

THANKS FOR THE GAME

The Best of Golf with
HENRY COTTON

Sidgwick & Jackson
London

First published in 1980 in Great Britain by
Sidgwick and Jackson Limited

Copyright © 1980 by Henry Cotton

Designed by Paul Watkins

ISBN 0 283 98640 9

Printed in Great Britain
by The Garden City Press Limited
Pixmore Avenue, Letchworth, Herts SG6 1JS
for Sidgwick and Jackson Limited
1 Tavistock Chambers, Bloomsbury Way
London WC1A 2SG

Preface

After over fifty years in the game, as a professional, championship winner and teacher, I feel I have earned the right to speak my mind on the game of golf, hoping that my words will reach at least some of the twenty million or so people throughout the world who enjoy, and sometimes suffer from, their involvement in this greatest of all sports.

Many years ago, when I first talked theory with the great Harry Vardon and asked him to write down what he had learned from a lifetime of golfing experience, he said, 'I have tried on several occasions, but whenever I read through what I have written it all seems so elementary: I can't help thinking that anyone not knowing that much already should not be playing the game.' Another old friend, Reginald Whitcombe, youngest of the three famous golfing brothers, took up his pen after winning the 1938 Open Championship and chose as his title, *Golf's No Mystery*. Like Vardon, Reg stressed the fundamental simplicity of the game, even to the point of implying that all the player had to do was pick up the club and thrash the ball by instinct. Two champions with a common theme: simplicity.

And now I too have been in the game for so long, and have learned from a life that has passed all too quickly that to play good golf rests entirely on the ability to find the back of the ball with the club head square. Much is written and talked about the complexities and subtleties of this or that technique. Great importance is placed on the need for a classical swing or on playing 'square to square'. Students everywhere seem to agonize over the finer points of the swing, or the position of the feet, or whether the head is quite still. All this emphasis on method: no mention of simply finding the ball – which is a development of a skill we all have from the day we are born. Small wonder that so many of today's club golfers

There never was a more ambitious golfer than Cotton, nor one more absorbed in all the manifold ways of golf as a profession. He devoted himself to the cause of technical perfection and success with an intensity that even Hogan hardly surpassed
PAT WARD-THOMAS

are tense and frustrated, worrying about details of method instead of simply getting out there on the course and enjoying this marvellous game, playing more by instinct than by theory.

My writing, my teaching, indeed the aim of this book, is to help people discover the joy in playing golf well. I love the game. It has given me a wonderful life, and I enjoy nothing better than to see others getting the same fun and excitement out of it. My beliefs and my methods have at times been considered antiquated, particularly by power-players and disciples of the so-called 'modern method', but I am happy to let results speak for themselves. While pupils of the modern school often work away endlessly because they are seeking one method only, with little or no improvement to reward them, my own pupils are relaxed, confident and see their game improving from the moment they start. 'Square to square' is fine for the power players who hit the ball so far they are in danger of hitting it out of play. Their need is to guide the ball so they push the shot rather than whip it. But how many golfers are power players? Very few. The vast majority, of course, need extra length. For them, better golf – and more enjoyable golf – comes from hitting the ball more consistently.

I have seen champions come and go like the short-lived daffodils and bluebells. Wine, women and song, and various other extravagances, have helped some on their way out of the headlines but for most the decline has been due simply to a lack of understanding of how to protect their talents from the ravages of time. Just a few, the truly great players, endure. They know their game, have good physiques, strong nerves, self control, a method they can rely on – and the sense to realize that the body changes with every tick of the clock. Many players alas believe that the technique they used in their 'finest hours' will be the key to

success forever, and even when they lose form they reach back into the past, studying films of themselves in a vain hope of recapturing something which has gone. It cannot work, it has gone for ever. To be a lasting success a player must adapt his play to his changing body, using his years of experience and his knowledge of his own game to maximize his strengths. The 'elder statesmen' of golf today can still play a fine round, but it is not the game they played in their mid-twenties. It applies to every sport!

For years I have suffered the nonsense inflicted on a gullible golfing world by 'experts' – both acknowleged and self-appointed. I always expected that my teacher should at least be able to show me what I wanted, and needed, to learn. I felt that unless an instructor was capable of

demonstrating precisely and impressively the shot he was asking me to make, then his advice was at best suspect. How I bristled when I heard, as we all did too often fifteen to twenty years ago, that 'You *must* have a square-to-square action'. Instructors can do untold harm drumming this maxim into entire classes. For what happens? One pupil in a hundred will play better golf. For the rest the results will range from frustration at best to slipped discs and strained muscles at worst. It is rarely mentioned now! No one method is right for every player. No single way of swinging a club can possibly work for the tall, the short, the fat, the thin, the weak and the powerful. All that counts in golf is to find the back of the ball squarely with the middle of the club face. Any style or method will do, and if it enables a player to strike the ball hard, square and consistently then it is a good swing, no matter how it may depart from the 'classical'.

Even some of our greatest professionals seem to me to be way off the mark in their theories. It makes me shudder to hear certain players declaring, 'Power is supplied by your legs, not by your hands.' How can they say this when they are quite capable of hitting a ball 200 yards while standing on one leg? While Bob Toski, one of America's best and most popular teachers, demonstrates a 200-yard drive while sitting on a chair.

Sixty years ago I remember that outstanding instructor Seymour Dunn proclaiming that golf was 85 per cent hands and only 15 per cent body. Nothing in a lifetime's experience in golf has happened to make me think otherwise. How right he has been! The body action used by many players today – all knees and stomach – came into prominence when the strong men of the past attacked the large ball which, in those days, tended to balloon when struck really hard. This action is a means of forcing the ball to

follow a low trajectory. It is a magnified push shot requiring more power than the ordinary player has at his command. It is still useful to the big power-men, but has no place in the repertoire of the average golfer.

When I started playing golf seriously I was not a big hitter and so my golf thinking and my methods were directed at ways of achieving greater length and consistently good length. Nothing has ever caused me to waver from my belief that this comes from the ability to find the back of the ball with the club face every time and from a fast whipping action of the club head at impact. Finding the ball requires only that a player develop a talent he already has. There is no magic involved. Few people have any difficulty in driving a nail squarely into a piece of wood. Why then make a complicated thing of hitting a ball? The golf club is admittedly a rather more unwieldy weapon than a hammer but the instinct is there and simply needs training. Even infants hit square when they slap at a ball with the open palm. As for that club head speed, all depends on the hands – strengthened individually using the tyre-practice described in this book and trained to work in complete harmony. Many of the old champions stressed that 'when your legs go, you are through winning'; Sam Snead during his 1979 trip to Australia announced that he was almost through with competing in the 'big leagues' for his legs had gone, and of course strong legs *are* essential for control. Accept this as a fact, learn to use the hands properly, and like me you will enjoy a lifetime of pleasure-golf.

Henry Cotton
Penina 1980

Introduction

Improving at Golf – Easily and Certainly

I always had a competitive spirit, that spirit that urges one to want to beat every opponent. When I first began to try to play golf well I realized that whilst a fierce desire to win, which unfortunately cannot be taught, was important, a good game was equally important and could be learned. I did not want to be a short accurate player, but a long accurate one.

As soon as I saw the big players in action I realized I was not strong enough 'through the ball', and I began to search for ways to build up my attack on the ball. But I found there was no information to be obtained on building up golfing muscles. 'Swing a heavy club or three clubs held together' was about all I could find. This was a start and I followed the advice, but with no 'contras', i.e. no left-hand swings. I found that this drill not only stretched my muscles, which was good I guess, but alas it also gave my back an unhealthy jerk which only added to the deformation of my spinal column which long hours of hitting golf shots in the normal right-shoulder-down position had produced. Now I have definitely decided that contras are as essential as normal swinging of the club to make successful golfers. Why do golfers so often play better after a rest? Because their spine and golf muscles have had a chance to get back to their normal condition and the one-sided deforming pull on the body has been stopped. The modern golf swing is not a natural sort of action; if it were instinctive there would not be so much advice about how to play the game.

When a person turns to golf, he or she is told that one certain series of movements must be learned before he or she can play, and all the standard jargon is trotted out. Learn the swing first and then 'we can try with the ball'! I taught this way for years, but at least I tried to get my pupils to strengthen their arms and hands. This was done hitting balls one-handed, hitting and then stopping the arms, hitting deep into the sand and through long grass, as well as lifting a heavy Indian club up and down, with the forearms resting on the arm of a chair or on a table. These exercises were valuable and helped me to build up my own game and that of many of my pupils too. But they did not really achieve what I wanted. I was seeking some greater resistance to the club than the impact of the golf ball itself. Swinging the club head through a trough full of oil or treacle or some other heavy liquid occurred to me, but I did not pursue that idea, it would be a bit too messy I feared. In all the instructional books the accent was still on the angle of the left wrist at the top or the positioning of the ball at address and other trivialities. This did not help to make a golfer a stronger player. So many went into the game as short players and stayed that way, to become good 'little' players, always victims of the good 'big' players. Then I discovered the value of a tyre.

The Importance of Showing Your Back to the Target

The photographs of Tony Lema and Arnold Palmer were taken by me when I played with them in a practice round prior to the Piccadilly World Matchplay Tournament at Wentworth in 1964. The players are on the 16th hole, which has become celebrated in recent times as a television 'disaster hole'. It is interesting to note that both stars are caught at the same moment in the backswing. Lema has the club face quite shut, but his left wrist is well under the shaft – an unusual combination. Palmer has the face not quite so shut, but his left wrist seems to be more in line with the forearm, not nearly so far under the shaft. Where exactly the hands are placed at the top of the backswing depends, as you can see, on the characteristics of the player's wrists.

Palmer has a little more shoulder turn than Lema; his chin is pointing at the ball and the hips are turned more. What, I think, will surprise some people who don't think the hips turn very much in modern golf is that both players have lifted the left heel to help their shoulder turns. And, as you can see, there is quite some strain on the back as the shoulders are twisted. However, I also have many photographs of Palmer with both feet flat on the ground at this point in the swing, so clearly the foot action varies according to the lie of the ground and the requirements of the individual shot.

The action of completing a full pivot is seen in the play of *all* good golfers. Some achieve this with both feet planted firmly on the ground; others need just an easing of the left foot from the turf; and there are those who need to raise the left heel quite considerably. It all depends on the general flexibility of the individual. My advice is that unless the spine is very free, and the muscles holding it very strong, players should avoid the modern tight wind-up of the trunk. And in any case players should remember to do contra exercises if they play and practise excessively. Keeping the legs as straight as possible when bending down to tee up the ball is always worth doing. Sam Snead prided himself on being able to pick his ball out of the hole with his legs straight. Full left-handed swings also help to ease the back for right-handed players and this is especially important for those who do a great deal of chipping and putting.

Charles Wood

James Adams

In the actions of the top players the left shoulder invariably points at the ball and the chin rubs against the sweater or shirt at the shoulder in a full swing. Lady golfers often leave a lipstick trace on the left shoulder, whilst the stubble on a man's chin can even rub a hole in a sweater.

How the hands hold the club face at the top – open, shut, or somewhere in between – depends on the strength of the player, the type of shot demanded and the loft and lie of the club face itself.

Do not always ground the club for your tee shots. Have the club head floating in the air behind the ball or even slightly above the level of the ball if you tend to hit the ground before the ball.

When driving from an elevated tee, pick out a distant object to aim at. Anything at eye level will serve – a tree, a roof-top, a hill top or even a cloud.

For a long sand shot get the ball near your right toe and hold the right leg completely stiff. Play the ball hard with 'wooden' wrists and a forceful follow-through.

Norman Sutton

Balance...Rhythm...Power
The Jack Nicklaus Method

There is no doubt that this husky American from Ohio has proved himself over the past two decades to be one of the most complete golfers of all time. He has everything – including an immense natural power that was carefully guarded and then harnessed. Even as a teenager he could hit the ball out of sight, and he had a poise, and a degree of concentration and determination, that few golfers in the history of the game have ever acquired. A happy married life with a beautiful schoolgirl friend contributed to his progress from outstanding amateur to top-ranking professional. He still has one of the most individual swings in the game. The club is taken high above the head, as high as is possible at the top – not a textbook position perhaps, for many great players, including Sam Snead, Ben

Hogan and Gary Player, have found it impossible to get their hands anywhere near as high as Nicklaus has been able to do. His surprisingly small hands make him favour the interlocking grip, which curiously suits very few players, though many have tried it and still do try it through being inspired by his successes. I cannot make the interlocking grip work for myself – it 'breaks' my fingers – but I never discourage pupils from trying it.

In the course of winning some £2 million in official prize money Nicklaus has made various small changes to his method. He has varied the amount he lifts his left heel in the backswing – from no lift at all when pitching to a very marked lift when using the driver. Once he starts down, however, all fits into the most classical of

positions in the important impact area. His wrists are not too flexible. Perhaps he has not tried to make them so, as I did as a boy and, I feel, succeeded. He tries to keep them wooden.

In this wedge shot sequence, during which he was playing into a wind, the requirement was clearly a 'push' shot. I took these pictures and was able to watch how he deliberately delayed the 'release of the hands' until after impact in order to keep the ball low. This is an easy stroke for most players to do for this length of shot, but Nicklaus is so strong that he can also achieve the same 'impact area' wrist action when driving. Unless you are a power golfer my advice to you is to reserve this action for push shots with lofted clubs only, or for a recovery from under a tree when the ball has to be kept low.

How the Hands Work

Handicap golfers who are fortunate enough to have professional coaching very quickly come to appreciate the importance of the role played by the left arm in the golf swing. There is no escaping the fact that if the left arm does not hold firmly to its path, the shot will be either misdirected or missed entirely.

As a youth I set about strengthening my arms and hands as I soon realized how weak they were in the crucial hitting area, and even today I spend as much time as possible on maintaining the tone of my arm muscles. Age may have taken its toll generally, but with a little extra exercise the arm muscles tone up considerably and the one-handed shots with a No. 4 iron, shown here, still carried well over 100 yards without too much effort.

The trick, if it can be called a trick, about the role of the left arm lies in what happens to the head of the club at the start of the downswing. Rather than stop dead at the top of the backswing and then start its downward path along exactly the same arc, the club head, in the case of most top golfers, can be seen to drop backwards, away from the golfer's head, as it starts its downward path. This backward movement of the club head is an insurance against its arc drifting outside the ball-to-hole line. In other words, the club head is kept firmly on the 'inside-to-out' line.

It comes as a surprise to many players to learn that the hooked shots sometimes played by very powerful players are caused by the left arm, not the right. Poor golfers often slice because of an untrained right hand, but the good player hooks through too much left-arm domination and not vice versa as is often suggested. John Panton from Glenbervie, a very good player all his life and usually very straight, had a slight tendency to hook his tee shots – these were *left*-handed hooks.

This series of photographs of myself, taken at Deauville, illustrates nicely the path of the club head and the action of the left hand. In the first, notice how I have already begun to pull the left arm down and how the club head has fallen back at the start of the downstroke. In the second, the wrist is preparing to 'flick' the club head, but despite the natural unwinding of the shoulders the club head has not crept forward. In the third,

with the club shaft almost horizontal, the back of the hand begins to turn in to the ball – one of the crucial points in the stroke.

I think *all* good golfers have had this action of the left hand; it is not new. If the shot is to be pushed the hand remains ahead of the ball at impact. If an ordinary shot is required, then the wrist can be allowed to 'throw' or 'flick' the club. This control of the freedom of the left hand, especially at impact, requires great strength and it is not generally known that Gary Player, who has called great attention to his own left arm action, is a naturally powerful left-handed athlete. A tendency to hook, which was always his problem, comes from his left arm action and not from his powerful right arm.

In the fourth photograph I have hit past my head and the right side has gone under, but note also in the fifth, at the end of a right-hand-only swing, how much *more* the body has gone round for the same degree of follow-through. In the sixth, a two-handed shot position just before impact, look for the bent right arm. This bent position is a feature of every good golfer's technique: the rabbit (novice) hits with a straight right arm – which is fatal.

Working on the right and left hands separately can, at times, be hard work, but as an exercise for improving both strength and accuracy there is none better and it is surprising just how quickly the arms can be educated. After the initial mis-hits the hands soon begin to 'find' the ball; then they are asked to work together, and that feeling of improved power is ample reward.

I doubt whether anyone has devoted as many back-breaking, hand-smarting, brain-tiring hours to the acquiring of golfing shots as has Cotton
BERNARD DARWIN

A Secret Mission with the Duke of Windsor

My sixty years of golf, starting alongside my father on a London course which sadly no longer exists, the Honor Oak and Forest Hill, have been filled with countless marvellously friendly matches and the most intense challenges. Naturally many have faded from my memory, but some remain as fresh in detail as if they had been played only yesterday.

One such vivid memory recalls a day in November 1938 when a four-ball game on the St Cloud course in Paris involved me in a moment of British history. It all begun with a message from my good friend Max (later Sir Max) Aitken who explained that the Duke of Windsor had asked for a meeting in Paris where he and the Duchess were living in exile following his abdication. He was anxious to get a true picture of public feeling at home in Britain. Could he seriously consider returning? The Duke thought that Max, being a young man and the son of Lord Beaverbrook, the newspaper baron, would have the pulse of the nation and would be able to offer a valuable opinion.

Max decided that in the circumstances it would be wrong to give their meeting the appearance of an organized, sombre affair. The best way to disguise it, he thought, would be for them to meet on a golf course, They both loved the game, and so arrangements were made. I readily accepted Max's invitation to make up a four with Percy Boomer, the St Cloud Golf Club professional, and left Bordeaux, where I was buying some wine for my cellar, for Paris and what was to prove an historic event.

We all met at St Cloud after lunch. I partnered the Duke against Max and Boomer, and we enjoyed our game in the most peaceful surroundings. Hardly another soul was to be seen, and we went unrecognized. We had tea in the clubhouse at the finish and then, with Boomer, I left the Duke and Max to talk in private. The outcome was that Max advised against an attempt to return to live in Britain. He explained that there were still certain areas of antagonism which simply wouldn't allow it to work. I'm sure Max was right, and the Duke obviously appreciated his advice.

The Duke was a keen golfer, and took the trouble to be professionally coached. I gave him advice from time to time and he applied himself

well, but he was never really strong enough to be a solid striker of the ball. The picture of him dressed in the golf outfit of the day, his cap made of the same tweed as the suit, was taken when he was Prince of Wales. The 'head down' position shows that he listened too well to his coach, though the artificial follow-through is strictly for the camera. Later, for a game in Vienna, he appeared in Bermuda shorts and a short-sleeved shirt; a trend-setter both on and off the golf course!

I liked the Duke and he was always extremely friendly towards my wife Toots and myself. He enjoyed speaking to Toots in Spanish and whenever he saw us he would approach, say 'Hello, señora', and converse in quite reasonable Spanish. He was a good friend of professional golf, and through Archie Compton did much with a single act to break down the barriers that

Funny the way the wheel always seems to turn. Now it looks as though in the States they are going to look for simple golf courses, avoiding those vast expensive to upkeep sand bunkers. Then, it is said, there is going to be a return to the original old-type clubhouse, a sports pavilion type with the simplest of services, to cut down the ever growing cost of luxurious country club memberships.

A Tip from the Top – from Tom Watson. 'Cotton said to me one of the things which caused me to swing badly on occasions was that I was not getting off my left heel on the backswing. My left knee was going straight out towards the ball instead of turning inwards. He told me to lift my left heel slightly before I took the club away and feel that left knee trying to go in just a little bit.' Watson continued, 'The left knee going in is the effect, not the cause of a good swing but it makes the turn a whole lot easier!'
This tip worked for Watson, but has now possibly outlived its usefulness. In much the same way Gary Player had a period of unsuccessful play, when he used my tip of holding his left heel clear of the ground throughout his swing to enable him 'to kill the ball' with his right hand and so stop his hook.
This 'left-heel-up' also cures a slice. Why? Because it checks the body unwind and allows the player to square up the club face at impact with his right hand, without the body interfering.

existed from the early days between pros and amateurs. There are a number of stories of how, as the dashing young Prince of Wales, he took Archie, a huge craggy-faced fellow, six feet four inches tall, to a posh London-area club for a game and how the secretary drew attention to the rule barring professionals from the clubhouse. The Prince politely said that if Archie couldn't be his guest inside the club then they would have to go elsewhere to lunch together; and off they went. That was the end of the incident, but it was the beginning of the breakthrough which eventually led to clubhouses being opened to professionals. So the professional golfer of today has much to thank the Duke for and I only wish that my 'secret mission' could have contributed to a happier outcome for himself and the Duchess.

17

Educate Your Hands at Cotton's University

When I was quite young one of my greatest idols was Abe Mitchell – a man with a casual yet masterly swing and a totally individual dress sense. His playing outfit usually consisted of a tight fitting tweed jacket, neat plus-fours with immaculate creases down the front, a matching cap, and beautifully polished expensive brown shoes. The very picture of sartorial elegance. The group photograph, taken at Coulsden Court in 1928, shows, left to right, my brother Leslie, myself, Charles Whitcombe, and Abe Mitchell.

He would walk on to the first tee as though dressed for a day's shooting, pick his hickory-shafted driver out of the bag, have one practice swing. Then he would take the club to the full horizontal position at the top, and with a terrific flash of the hands drive the ball up to 300 yards down the course. He would finish with the club shaft round the body at waist level. Abe did this time after time; it all seemed so simple. He tried

to play with the steel shaft but could never play as well with it as with hickory; I think he missed the torsion of the wooden shaft. If a weak spot ever appeared in his game it was usually on the greens because he was highly strung and used to get anxious, especially if kept waiting. But I dreamed of one day having hands and wrists that would enable me to do what he did with the clubhead: swish it through the ball with a piercing whistle. So I tried and tried, and practised day and night until I realized that just swinging a golf club and hitting golf balls wasn't enough. I was getting better, but too slowly. Abe had been a gardener as a young man and hard manual work had given him tremendously strong arms and hands and a tough yet supple back. I decided then that I too needed a stronger drill.

I had concentrated on playing and practising golf seriously since I was about sixteen and looking back I realized I should have done other

exercises. I ought to have carried on playing football and cricket, and gone on building my body in the gym, and done more running. So I began thinking of what I could do to drive the ball further and develop a faster impact. I finally hit on the idea of swinging in long grass as a way of offering greater resistance to the club head. I used to go to a quiet spot on the golf course and swing away for hours in the deepest rough I could find, using the club head like a scythe. It took some doing, and was extremely hard work, but it worked: I began to win tournaments.

Then golf courses became more manicured. There was less long grass and I couldn't find enough 'hay' to mow. When I had practised for years hitting the ball one handed using each hand in turn, my left hand became so 'well educated' that I could use it alone to hit a four-wood 'off the deck' almost 200 yards every time.

But with the long grass needed for practice becoming more and more difficult to find I had to discover a suitable substitute. Then one day at Temple, near Maidenhead, my home club at the time, I parked my car right behind the professional's shop and saw an old motor tyre lying abandoned on the ground. Whoever dumped it there had no idea of the contribution he was unwittingly to make to the game of golf! I gave the tyre a good kick to move it out of the way and it suddenly occurred to me that this was the thing to hit with a golf club to strengthen and educate the hands. I popped into my shop, selected an old iron, and set about striking the tyre. It worked so well that I had mixed feelings: I was delighted to have made the discovery, but regretted it had come so late, for by this time I had practically retired from competitive golf.

In 1968 I finally moved to live and work in Penina, Portugal, where two years earlier I had

And so, step by step, going on his rather lonely way, undeterred by criticism and unwavering in hard resolve, Cotton built himself up into a remarkable figure, one which to the man in the street stands for golf in a way that no other in this country has quite done since the days of Harry Vardon
BERNARD DARWIN

completed building the new course. Pupils, and promising amateurs wanting to turn pro, took to the new exercise with enthusiasm and news of its value quickly spread through the golfing world. The 'tyre drill' certainly developed strength and flexibility but I also wanted to achieve greater *speed* through the impact area. So, using a steel golf shaft without a head, but with a grip, I devised a set of exercises involving a fast to-and-fro whipping action inside the tyre. As the headless club could be moved to and fro so much faster than a real club, overall speed of action was improved, but perhaps more important, the pupil could concentrate on taking the full shock of impact on the hands, while maintaining a tight grip on the club, but *without* slowing down the speed of the club head.

Many players seem to relax the hands at impact because if they grip too tightly they slow the action. But if they hold the club loosely it tends to slip. It is all a question of finding the optimum grip required to keep the club head moving fast while retaining strength enough to avoid mis-hitting if you do fail to make contact with the dead centre of the club face.

The tyre drill is now a ritual for me. A few blows at a time are enough and then it is a matter of recognizing any weak points and working on them – educating the hands to complement each other so that they work in harmony. Some people will whack the tyre too often or for too long, not realizing how tired they are becoming – and then immediately go out to play a game only to find they are not striking the ball well. Muscles need hard exercise, but they also need a period of rest before being asked to perform at peak. Working out a practice routine to suit your individual game is one of the secrets of success.

Too often I have seen young players rush to the practice ground in a panic to try to find their game, having arrived on the day of the match with no confidence in their play. Despite all the practice they have put in beforehand they just cannot find those vital straight shots. The reason is that the hands are fighting each other. Not a lot perhaps, but enough. They go to the practice ground, hit the first few shots off target, anxiety and tension creep in, and they find themselves walking to the first tee tired and confused, not knowing what swing to use or what is going to happen to the ball. Really they should already have the game – and bring it to the practice ground simply to get the feel of the club in their hands. If it doesn't work then, perseverance, concentration and a cool head are needed. Anyone can score when all is going well: it is the mark of a good player – and a characteristic of *every* great player – to 'get it round', somehow, even when things are going badly.

I discovered early in my career that on arriving at a tournament, if I hadn't brought my game with me I certainly wouldn't find it by working frantically on the practice ground. I too got desperate when things would not come right, but it was not that I did not know how to play; the problem would invariably be more to do with muscles being in poor shape, or simple fatigue. The individual must find his own balanced blend of rest and practice. Some players try a long rest, without play, and then get in a panic, thinking that they have lost their game. Others, like the Whitcombe brothers who were natural players, can leave their clubs untouched for weeks and then go out and set a new course record. I have been fortunate; I had a gift for the game. But I had to work hard to become a strong player and that hard work, and my continuing regular drill, keeps me still hitting the ball quite well – even at my age.

In heavy rough where the long blades of grass tend to cling round the neck of the club, it is very important to hold tightly and to anticipate that the blade will twist readily on contact with grass and ball. Severiano Ballesteros must be the best player out of the rough since Arnold Palmer : he hits the ball tremendous distances from seemingly impossible lies in the 'jungle'.

If you are scared of your approach shots, and either hit them thin or go soft on them too often, aim to strike half an inch into the ground behind the ball.

One of the toughest situations in the game is to find yourself playing into the wind or with the wind off the left side. There is a great temptation to fight the wind rather than use it. If you fight the wind you obviously lose distance ; far better to go with it, letting the ball fade into play if the layout of the hole allows.

Cliff Michelmore demonstrating the tyre drill

Locke Won The Open Yet Nearly Lost It!

Photographic evidence of an incident that could have rocked the golfing world. Here you see the old master Bobby Locke, at the request of his partner Bruce Crampton (standing on the right), marking his ball after playing a marvellous second shot at the last hole of The (British) Open at St Andrews in 1957. He had a five to win and had put his controlled hooked second shot, which travelled almost over Tom Morris's golf shop right out of bounds and back, to this distance from the flag, four to five feet.

Well, there he is putting down the disc to mark his ball, at Crampton's request, one club-head's length away from where it came to rest. That gave Crampton a clear putt without the ball-marker being in the way. Crampton putted out and then Locke replaced his ball. With two putts to win, from just five feet, the title was virtually his. And yet he still had a chance to lose it and if somebody had spoken up at the time, he *could* have lost it!

Why? Because, as these stills from a news film show, he replaced the ball on the marker instead of one club-head's length away, which he *should* have done to replace it in the identical position. He holed the putt and won The Open by three shots. It wasn't until much later that an official remembered seeing him replace the ball in the wrong position. Of course it was an innocent mistake, but it could have caused trouble. Quite a discussion followed but it was rightly decided that Locke had won the championship, and anyway he had been presented with the Cup, and that should be the end of it. It was a fair decision but the runner-up, Peter Thomson, might have left the course feeling slightly aggrieved. Playing strictly by the book there had of course been a clear infringement of the rules.

Walter Hagen

Walter Hagen was another of my heroes. I keep using the word hero, but he was the fellow who made me think, 'That's what I want to do. I want to be like "The Haig". I want to have silk shirts with monograms, and two-toned shoes, beautifully made suits and gold cuff-links.' What an impression he made, arriving at golf clubs in Rolls Royces which he rented, of course, when in Britain. That really was something in those days, right after the First World War.

I got to know Hagen in America. I went over as a young pro in November 1928 to play the winter tour with the best pros of the U.S.A. When in California the pros used to have their headquarters in the Hollywood Plaza, Los Angeles, which was a new hotel at that time. Two dollars fifty a night for room and bathroom – and the dollar was then five to the pound! I remember still as if it happened yesterday how, after one particular tournament, Walter's manager Bob Harlow paid the bill for Hagen and himself out of a suitcase full of dollar bills which he dumped on the cashier's counter. The cash represented the proceeds from exhibition matches played on the route from Detroit (Hagen's home town) to California. Bob collected the money at the 'gate' – but somehow never found time to count it. The bills weren't even in bundles and he went through the suitcase like a ferret, looking for twenty and fifty dollar bills, leaving the smaller ones in the bottom of the case like confetti. Then off they went to the next venue. Life was casual all right.

Walter had an open tourer, a Stutz 'Bearcat' – one of the most expensive cars of the day – and off he would go, not really worried whether he had finished well or otherwise in the tournament. I recall one tournament at which he won a prize and a law officer stepped out of the crowd to say, 'I'll take that cheque.' It was for owed alimony. Hagen just roared with laughter. He lived well and he is supposed to be the first golf pro to make a million and spend it, and in those days a million dollars was a real fortune.

He won our Open in 1922 (I was only fifteen at the time), in 1924, 1928 and in 1929 when I actually played with him, on the final day that year at Muirfield. We had already become very good friends, despite our age difference of fifteen years, and that year he went on to play in Paris

with his Ryder Cup Team in a triangular sort of match, British and French pros competing. Britain had won the Ryder Cup match at Moortown Golf Club, Yorkshire, the second of the series, and it was a great thrill for me, for when I won my match, playing No. 7 in the singles, the Ryder Cup was ours.

Hagen was still making big money and spending most of it while living life to the full. One day I said to him, 'I would love to have one of your clubs.' 'What club would you like?' he answered. They were all hickory shafts then and I had fancied a No. 8 of today from his bag marked, then, a 'mashie niblick'. He said, 'Come and pick it up some time,' and so whilst in Paris I went to Claridges in the Champs Elysées where he was staying, telephoned his room, and was invited to 'Come on up, Kiddo'. He had a suite of connecting rooms, something like 407 to 415, so I went to 407, knocked on the door and when there was no answer to my 'Hello?' I pushed open the door. Inside was a girl wearing a negligee. 'Mr Hagen?' I enquired. She appeared not to know who he was, but indicated that I should go to the next room. To my great embarrassment – I was a fairly innocent 22-year-old chap – I then went through a whole series of rooms, one after the other, all full of half-dressed

Cotton wore Savile Row clothes and silk monogrammed
shirts. He drove a large motor car – which he had a
tendency to park opposite signs saying 'No Parking'
HENRY LONGHURST

young ladies! I eventually found Walter lying on
his bed with the telephone still in his hand. He
hadn't put it down after speaking to me and he
was fast asleep! I wasn't surprised that he was
exhausted! I didn't know what to do, but there
were a whole lot of clubs in one corner and
obviously he had sorted some out. As he was
soon to depart for America, by ship of course, I
didn't want to wake him, so I helped myself to
an 8 iron, left a goodbye and thank you note
and went quietly away.

Walter loved playing golf, he had played
baseball as a young man and had a natural gift
for hitting a ball. He played from a very wide
stance with rather a lurch, which people
criticized, but *he* knew what he was going to do
with it. Of course, he used to make mistakes but
I think he almost welcomed them as he enjoyed
the extra challenge and showmanship of
producing a great recovery.

The picture of him putting was taken at
Sandwich in 1922; it was 'that for The Open',
the first time Hagen took the championship. It is
interesting because the ball has not yet reached
the hole but he has played that stroke quite a bit
with his right shoulder, and, after striking the
ball, he has immediately lifted his club as if
finishing an approach. Today, if a fellow had got
the ball on the way to the hole like that you
would probably find his head still firmly down
and he'd have played it with a definite method.
But of course this was long ago. In those days
Hagen used a blade putter with a rather flat lie
and with the ball opposite his left toe; but on
this occasion it seems as if he's deliberately tried
to top the ball and make it run extra well.

Walter died a few years ago having seen, of
course, the arrival of the jet aeroplane. I always
wonder just what he would have made out of
golf if he could have fitted more events into his
life. His classic remark, 'So many people today
never have time to stop off and smell the flowers
as they go through life', is truer than ever.

The photograph of him sitting at lunch, a
flower in his buttonhole and two footmen
waiting on him, was taken in 1937 at Sir Philip
Sassoon's Trent Park home, the first place the
Americans of the Ryder Cup Team visited after
coming off the boat-train from Southampton
that year. There was a super 9-hole golf course in

the grounds on which they 'fooled around' to get
rid of their sea legs and then followed a fabulous
lunch – a picture of gracious living in which
Walter was in his element.

Hagen travelled the world with Joe Kirkwood,
Joe very often giving a 'trick shots' show. Then,
for a change, he went on another round-the-
world trip with young Horton Smith, an
American boy-wonder professional whose career
was tragically cut short when his wrist was
broken in an accident in a friend's car. He
played many matches partnering Hagen, and the
old master would just let Horton 'ride along', as
before his accident Horton was a *wonderful*
player. His putter was a magic wand with which
he won seven out of the first eleven tournaments
on the 1928–9 tour.

In those early days the pros had agreed to give
ten per cent of their winnings to form the
players' winter circuit of tournaments – I chipped
in my bit – and Bob Harlow, Hagen's manager,
became the first tour manager, a sort of
honorary job then. Hagen did not win very much
in that period but he used to say, 'I'm having a
wonderful time and they can't take that away
from me.' That was his philosophy. He did the
most gracious things. If you said you admired his
cardigan and he had another one handy, he
would probably give it to you off his back.

I don't know how he managed, but his
trousers were always beautifully pressed and on
the course he was always immaculately turned
out. It's not so easy today because you can't get
any laundry done and everyone travels light.
Progress is a wonderful thing, but it can have its
disadvantages. Many professionals in recent
years have set out to imitate these elegantly
dressed stars of the old days, but they have failed
in my eyes for I have seen bright yellow slacks
with grease stains all over them and dirt all
round the pockets where the hands go in for the
peg tees. Such a thing would have horrified
Hagen.

Somebody once said when they saw this
picture of Hagen wearing a sunhat, 'What time's
the cricket match?' But he dressed as well for
comfort and that was the dress of the day, a big
brim on sunhats. Very elegant it was too. I don't
think we will ever have another Walter Hagen or
play in monogrammed silk shirts.

The King and I

People often ask me if I remember particular shots and incidents from past games. Some I do remember, others have faded a little; there have been so many games in sixty years of golf. But my own large collection of photographs, and the hundreds which have been sent to me over the years by friends and fellow golfers around the world, are a rich source of memories – each face, each green recalling half-forgotten details.

Some incidents, however, remain fresh in the mind without need for prompting, like this scene on the first tee of The Open at Muirfield in 1948. His Majesty King George VI is wishing me luck after shaking hands at the start of the second round. Our great golf scribe Bernard Darwin later wrote, 'With the Royal touch still fresh upon his hands. . .'

On the King's left is the Captain of the Club, Mr A. C. McLaren, and on my right is my partner Mr R. Pattinson, a club amateur who played really magnificently and finished the whole four rounds of the championship. Just a few minutes after this shot was taken I walked off the first green having hit my second shot, against the breeze, four yards past the flag with my No. 3 wood and knocked in the putt for a three – the start of my record round of 66. It proved to be a major step towards winning the title, which I did the following day when we played thirty-six holes. That final day was quite a test of stamina but a round then in a twosome took only two-and-a-half to three hours and I finally came home to win by five strokes with a score of 284.

An Inside Tip

All golfers know that a sliced ball is caused by the club head getting outside the ball-to-hole line at impact. They know that to avoid a slice the ball must be attacked on an inside-to-out path; but how much can a golfer get on the inside? Is there a limit?

Bobby Locke, a golfing hero of post-war days, had the most fabulous hooking flight on all his shots. He stood with a very closed stance at address, took the club head far round his body and despite returning to impact with a pronounced shoulder roll, which took the club head towards the ball-to-hole line on the way down, was still able to keep the club head attacking the ball on a very definite inside-to-out arc.

This proved one thing: there is no such thing as 'too much inside' on the way back. He hooked every shot, right through the bag; drove with a No. 2 wood, and played the most accurate wedge shots – all from his closed stance and with the inside-to-out attack.

I often have to 'sell' the closed stance to pupils who find difficulty in getting a full shoulder pivot in the backswing. The placing of the right foot back at address adds an appreciable amount to the width of the backswing and, of course, gets the club well on the inside right away.

One action is often missed in the study of the very-inside-out swing, and that is the use of the right shoulder to drive the blow forwards. Players using a flat swing also bring their hit at the ball to a forward attack. Not just to a grossly inside-to-out path, sliding the club face across the ball.

So many golfers, trying too hard to do everything right, somehow get their bodywork cramped as the right arm is made to push through too much *under* the head. The whole action is then devoid of power and somehow the attack on the ball is down, not through. The club head thuds into the turf just behind the ball which, when seen in a photograph or on film, looks quite good; yet the ball never travels well. It lacks punch.

It is perhaps dangerous to recommend a shoulder roll to any golfer for it is easy to do and can easily lead to exaggeration. And yet there are thousands of golfers 'locking' their swings and cramping their attack on the ball by

insisting on 'forcing' an under and through finish.

I think far too many golfers are conservative in this matter of the closed stance. They are shy about using it. They believe it is incorrect, a trick, part of two wrongs making a right. This is not so at all. It suits many players and yet is generally ignored. I find, too, that it helps many golfers in the short game, for they get an extra foot in length on the arc of the club in the backswing, for many short approaches are missed because the backswing is too short and then the shot is hurried. Experiment with a flatter backswing; it does no harm to find out which extremes give what.

An Unsung Hero!

Gleneagles

In 1951, when I was living at the Dorchester Hotel, I received a call from Sir Harry Methven who, among many other influential positions, had recently been appointed director of the newly-created Transport Hotels Commission, the body appointed for the direction of the hotels division of the nationalized railways. Sir Harry's brief from the Chancellor of the Exchequer, Sir Stafford Cripps, was to close down or sell off all loss-making operations.

Sir Harry, a charming old Scot, was crazy about golf and asked if he could come and see me to discuss a serious problem. Among the hotels marked down for disposal was Gleneagles Hotel in Scotland, and the Manor House Hotel at Moretonhampstead in Devon, both money-losers. I had never actually heard of the course and hotel at Moretonhampstead but Gleneagles Hotel I knew well and loved. Sir Harry said Gleneagles was losing money mainly because the season was too short, while at Moretonhampstead, in the home park of one of the Hambledon family's houses, the 'hotel' was considered too small ever to pay. I was asked what I thought could be done to save them.

The outcome of our first discussion was an agreement that Gleneagles could possibly be saved if the season could be extended by one month. At that time I had connections with the Saxone Shoe Company which marketed a very successful line of golf shoes under the trade name 'Gleneagles', so a link-up in some way struck me. I proposed establishing a new tournament, to be held in the third week of October. The newly nationalized railway hotels put up some of the necessary prize money; Saxone doubled it; and so was born the Gleneagles-Saxone Invitational Pro-Am Handicap Foursomes. The Highland Brigade's last week of the season's Jamboree and the Fishmongers Golfing Society both immediately and sportingly agreed to put the dates of their annual golfing events back a month and so almost within twenty-four hours we had ensured the survival of Gleneagles Hotel. The new Pro-Am tournament was to be held that very year.

It would have been tragic if Gleneagles Hotel had gone back to being an institution of some sort, which was quite on the cards, rather than remaining one of the world's greatest golfing centres. Things were happening so quickly during those early days of nationalization that if we had missed the opportunity then we could never have saved this great hotel and courses.

Shortly afterwards Sir Harry invited me to travel down to Devon and take a look at

Stoke Poges Golf Club

Moretonhampstead. 'Wherever is it?' I asked. I had been in golf then for so many years that it was hard to believe that there was a great course I had never visited. 'It's a beautiful golf course on the fringe of Dartmoor,' he said – and off we went for the day. To my delight I found a marvellous mansion house, sixty bedrooms converted into a hotel, with a full sized covered tennis court, squash courts, beautiful driveways, extensive gardens, and 18 holes of the most charming golf, with a trout stream running through the grounds and the course. It was losing at that time £6,000 a year and Harry said, 'Do you want to buy it? It is down for sale for £21,000.' Today that sounds so ridiculous that you might well ask why I didn't snap it up. But at that time I wasn't interested in owning a golf course; I was thinking more of easing up than of starting a whole new type of business. I said, 'The golf course and hotel are great, but there is no reason for the 18th hole to finish 500 yards from the clubhouse and the hotel.' As the first tee was at the bottom of the steps leading from the hotel lounge, which is ideal for a golf course, there was no reason not to have the 18th green on the other side, close to the building, too. This alteration I planned, and it was soon done.

I had been following golf all my life, and yet I never knew of this golfing paradise. So I said to Harry, 'As a start, why don't you recommend that they give cheap golfing weekends, advertised on posters at all the various Midland railway stations? Cost for the weekend, ten guineas; first class return railway fare and one (or two, I forget which) nights at the hotel, golf included.' Within two months the place was so booked up with people staying the weekend and then telling their friends, that this cheap programme had to be altered. It went back to a normal full-price golfing weekend, still giving some advantages of course. And it has never looked back. But one of my greatest regrets is that I didn't just say to the bank, 'Give me £21,000 and I'll buy it for myself.' We live and learn. Or do we?

Another missed opportunity dates from the same period and involved the beautiful Stoke Poges Club. Two hundred acres freehold, near Slough, scheduled green belt – and on sale for £30,000! I had an option for a week, but couldn't find anybody to help me, though I contacted many rich friends. They all said it was too much of a risk. So I didn't go on. Can you imagine that? It was finally bought by the local council, who rented the course and club to the original Stoke Poges Golf Club, and it thrives.

The Turn

Three Young Swings – Jack Nicklaus, Arnold Palmer and myself – and all horizontal. The big difference here is in the foot action. The shoulder turn is big for all three but the position of the right knee is quite different. I tend to straighten my right leg at the top of the swing while the other two players have a more 'sitting' position, with the right knee a little more bent. I lift my left heel, they play nearly flat-footed here, but the question is, 'Can the back stand the strain of that body twist forever?' I reduce the strain by turning my hip and my shoulder equally. A flat-footed action winds up the spine to get a recoil from the top down, whilst I am turning the whole of my body.

Note how all three of us have the ball well teed up, in my case positioned slightly more centrally than those of Nicklaus and Palmer. But the only thing that matters, as I always stress, is to bring the club head square to the ball at the moment of impact, and that I have succeeded in doing, more or less, for the last fifty years. I have generally used a full three-quarter length backswing, with my hands lower, not head-high as here, but at this particular period I hit the ball extra well.

Left: Jack Nicklaus   Above: Arnold Palmer

The Dormy House at Sunningdale

I enjoyed finding these pictures in my collection: Harry Bradshaw, Bernard Hunt, Fred Daly, and in the distance some other members of the 1953 Ryder Cup Team, of which I was proud to be the Captain. These boys would work very hard, 36 holes a day, getting ready for the match. At lunchtime between rounds we had a good meal; meat was still rationed, but people very kindly sent us steaks. We each had a glass of wine with every meal, because I thought that it was a good builder-up of nerves and strength. This was the result! They simply passed out, which must have been very good for their nerves in the end anyway, and 36 holes in a day was just a walk. We lost by only one point, so near and yet so far. I think they all enjoyed their week and the routine, which was tough, tough enough to make Fred Daly exclaim, 'I'm walking my legs off – almost down to my knees!'

Note Daly's firm reverse overlap with the index finger of the left hand; he was a wonderful finisher and despite seemingly endless waggles over the ball on the putting green, holed some historic putts.

Picking Up the Threads in 1945

The first tournament held after the war, the *News Chronicle,* was played in terrible weather at Brighton, on the exposed downland course of the Hollingbury Golf Club. I won the first prize, a cheque of £300 which in today's terms would be worth perhaps £3,000.

This picture amuses me because there I am receiving my cheque at the rear end of a lorry.

The scene is not like a golf prize-winning, more like an award at a farm show. I'm enjoying it obviously, but the general scene – kitchen steps and all – reminds me of an England still in austere times, as it was; petrol was rationed, food was rationed, and so were clothes, and were to remain so into the fifties. The golf balls were almost 're-moulds', certainly not very good.

Harry Vardon

Golfing history – the great Harry Vardon driving off the first tee at St Andrews before the First World War. The occasion must have been a practice round for The Open or some other tournament, otherwise I hardly think the crowd would have been allowed to block the view of the old members sitting in their armchairs in front of that famous window when the actual event started! Also in the picture is J. H. Taylor with his arms folded, playing in trousers. 'J. H.' never wore plus-fours; he reckoned his legs were too thick. In fact, you never see a group photograph showing J. H. Taylor seated with his legs crossed. He just couldn't cross his legs because of his enormously thick thighs.

Harry Vardon, playing in his usual rubber-soled shoes, has allowed his left foot to slew round. This was always one of his characteristics, and it is even used by players today. I certainly don't recommend it, but I do accept that it is safer to play this way than to lock the foot into the turf with very big shoe spikes – unless you have a very flexible ankle, as disc trouble is likely.

Harry always wore shallow stiff collars, as did all his colleagues at that time. I couldn't believe that there was any advantage in this, so one day I got one of these shallow collars, put it on, with a similar tie, and tried to play golf in it. To my delight and amusement, I found that when I twisted my body my clothes didn't go with me. Except for the fact that it's such an effort to get collars starched today, it's not a bad golf uniform! One wag has even suggested that the collar might go well with modern golfing dress! Bermuda shorts as a start!

Ken Brown

St Andrews

This is the young man most British pros would choose to have putting for them. But it's not just natural talent that makes this lanky young player so good: he putts and chips for three hours every day he can – and for a man of six feet two inches that is exhausting, back-breaking work.

All successful putters seem able to make the ball 'ring' off the putter blade and Ken is no exception. His rusty old-fashioned wry-necked blade with the short hickory shaft works wonders in the hands of this promising young player. Another fourteen pounds or so on his light frame would I think be a great help to his long game. Not that he is particularly short off the tee but he needs to really thrash the ball with his long irons in order to stay up with the power players. If you need woods for too many second shots it is hard to stay with the powerful hitters on the course and on the scoreboard. Ken disappointed us when he began to putt with a bronze-headed steel-shafted club; has his old favourite betrayed him?

A brutal fine by the P.G.A. for misdemeanours on and off the course during official team events, whilst they are not going to affect his living, may hurt his pride and confidence. I know he will soon forget these incidents and begin to conform with golfing etiquette and custom.

In Harry Vardon's great days, students of golf believed that his incredible accuracy off the tee came from a gift of being able to take up exactly the same address position time after time. Experiments proved otherwise. Playing from a bare tee, with no turf, and with the ball teed on sand (the wooden tee was not introduced until 1926) Vardon hit a series of apparently identical drives, and each time the precise position of his feet was recorded. The results proved that his feet were differently placed for each shot but the ball landed within feet of the target every time. His gift was to find the ball with the club face consistently and accurately no matter what the variation in his stance. Indeed, the head of his club was so shallow that not only did he have to guide it to the ball but he had to do so at exactly the right height in order not to sky the ball – and that I never saw him do.

TED RAY.

HARRY VARDON.

T. H. COTTON.

A Prize, value £5, for the best Title submitted for this picture.

J. H. TAYLOR.

JACK SMITH.

C. WHITCOMBE.

GAMAGES
GOLF WEEK
MARCH 19th—23rd.

¶ BE you "Rabbit" or "Tiger," or even trying to make up your mind to "take up" Golf, you MUST come to Gamages next week. Under the Great roof of the famous Gamage Sports Hall will forgather the Giants of the Game.

¶ A real Bunker and Putting Greens, of course ; and every modern gadget known to Golfers. The Putting Green will be made of special Cumberland Turf, the first of its kind ever laid in London for indoor Exhibition. Come and perfect your strokes and discuss your problems with such masters as :—

| J. H. TAYLOR | H. VARDON | TED RAY |
| H. COTTON | C. WHITCOMBE | J. SMITH |

GAMAGES
The World's Sports Specialists
HOLBORN, LONDON, E.C.1.

Not Allowed Now!

Golf Illustrated, 16 March 1928, carried a full-page advertisement announcing free golf lessons at Gamages store the following week. For five days Ted Ray, J. H. Taylor, Harry Vardon, Charles Whitcombe, Jack Smith and I could be found in a row of nets on the ground floor of the famous Holborn store: Taylor in the first net, the others in order of seniority, and myself, as the youngest, last in line.

It was a long week with a seemingly endless stream of people anxious to seek free advice on their game. One little fellow in a long raincoat and trilby hat kept coming back for more. He had a lesson with everybody – right down the line – until Taylor, a man known for his dry sense of humour, proposed that if he returned each of us should tell him something different.

Sure enough he was back again the next day, and so it started:

Taylor:	'You really must follow through as far as possible.'
Vardon:	'Now what is really wrong with your game is that you are overdoing the follow-through. You have to shorten that finish.'
Ray:	'Now mate, you're hitting too much from the top. You must watch it. Hit later!'
Whitcombe:	'You're doing fine. Now all you have to do is start hitting from the top.'

By this time the poor fellow must have been in a bit of a daze, but on he went – to Jack Smith, at that time by far the longest driver in the country, who was overheard to advise: 'You must make your left hand and arm do everything.'

Then to me for the final 'gem' of the day – the inevitable 'You've *got* to keep that left hand out of it.'

When last seen he was carrying his umbrella and raincoat and wandering out of the store with a glassy-eyed stare!

Not long after this incident the Professional Golf Association ruled against members being involved in such promotional efforts by stores and so the 'Golf Weeks' died.

Benno

At one period early in the war Benno Moiseiwitsch, one of the world's great pianists, rented a house across the road from my home 'Shangrila' at the entrance to Ashridge Golf Club, Hertfordshire. He was about to leave on a tour to entertain the Forces and asked us if we could look after a grand piano for him. As we had plenty of room I told him to bring it over. 'But there is a condition,' I said. 'Whenever you are practising, you must come and practise in our house.' He did, and what a delight it was to have music by Moiseiwitsch filling the whole of 'Shangrila', but I could only hear it once in a while alas. His favourite saying as a supreme pianist was, 'If I do not practise for one day, I know it. If I do not practise for three days the critics know it. And if I do not practise for a longer time, the public knows it.'

He played golf, but in a mediocre 18-handicap way. His real passion was, obviously, the piano and next was playing poker at the Savage Club in London when he could get a chance. Whilst a great piano player must have strong hands, wrists and forearms, he was not able to swing a golf club with the control and feel necessary to guide the club to the ball. Golf to him was always an adventure.

Fiddling With Golf Clubs

Here is a youthful Arnold Palmer at Royal Birkdale in 1961 on the way to winning his first British Open. He already had a great name in America, but this win enhanced his reputation as a world class golfer. It has perhaps been forgotten in the march of time that Dai Rees had to get down in two to tie with Palmer at the 72nd hole. Had he succeeded he would have changed history, but he went through the back of the green with his splendid second shot. His chip left him a five-foot putt which curled away to the right of the hole, and so he joined the band of 'unknown' runners-up. Only winners are remembered.

During that championship I remember seeing Palmer go into Bobby Halsall's pro shop (Bobby served the Royal Birkdale club for fifty years), put his driver in the vice with a bit of protective leather wrapped round the shaft, and then twist the head to 'lie off'. In other words, he deliberately put a slice angle on the club face. I was absolutely appalled. I didn't think anybody would be so brave as to risk a favourite driver in the vice – let alone in the middle of the Open Championship. But he had been hooking the ball quite a bit and had calculated that by opening up the face of the club a little he might cure the problem. And it did. He just went out and played super golf. What confidence!

A few professionals have earned reputations for 'fiddling' with golf clubs, but the need for this skill has lessened since the coming of self-adhesive lead tape strips. A length of this tape can be carried in the pocket or golf bag, enabling the player, while actually out on the course, to experiment with changes to the weight and balance of any club. Formerly any such experiments were slow, difficult, and risky, and had to be done by experts. To alter the balance of a wooden club required holes to be drilled to take molten lead, while changes to an iron club were nearly impossible, a big soldering job. Today a putter's feel, for example, can be altered in a moment to suit the speed of the greens, though such adjustments are not allowed during tournament play. I learned to make and repair clubs when at Fulwell Golf Club, Middlesex, where I was assistant No. 6 for nearly two years.

'Just look at this swing.' said the poor player to his pro. 'Every time I aim at a daisy, off comes its head. Look. I'll just do it once more.' And sure enough, off came the flower-head. 'But when I tee up the ball, and do exactly the same swing, just look what happens. Terrible. It goes nowhere. What should I do?'

The pro had been around for many years and drawing on his vast experience replied, 'Why not place the ball on a daisy?'

When Alfred Perry won the 1935 Open at Muirfield he played the last thirty-six holes with the same ball – a Dunlop 65. This, of course, must have happened before and since, but I doubt if one ball would today be used for even nine holes of a championship round. Some pros change the ball every three holes, or even sooner if it becomes scuffed in any way. What a difference in outlook.

The advice 'Keep your head steady and your eye on the ball' when putting can cause so much tension and restriction, and therefore nerves, that the ball is rarely struck properly. A true impact is essential. So if you are not getting a solid strike, let your right shoulder and head go through with the club.

I thought the full pivot so important that I used to write on the palm of my left glove, 'Turn, you idiot!' As it was a habit of mine always to pull my left glove firmly on to my hand just before I gripped the club, this little gem was always well in the forefront of my mind at the crucial moment.

Champion Women

I have followed women's golf all my life. Many top ladies have been my pupils and I have enjoyed playing with them and watching the best of them in action in competitions.

Doris Chambers was our Women's Champion in 1923. She was a big woman and dressed in the typical woman's gear of the time: felt hat; a shirt blouse; club tie; cardigan; and voluminous tweed skirt. Miss Joyce Wethered, later Lady Heathcoat-Amory, one of her contemporaries and one of the great lady golfers, used to wear skirts cut to the width of her stance. Nobody thought of it as being an artificial aid.

Then from a later generation came Pam Barton who was perhaps one of the first really powerful women golfers. In this photograph she is dressed in a pullover that I had designed and had made up for me by Jack Izod. He is still remembered in America, where his trademark is still known as Dozi! Jack was a West End men's outfitter and shirt-maker, then in Conduit Street, London, with great taste. He used to have made exclusively for him special heavy 5-ply cashmere sweaters in pastel shades and navy blue and he sold many to King George VI.

Pam, a girl prodigy in her day, who hit the headlines as a teenager, attacked the ball very, very hard. I played a lot of golf with her as she used to come and be coached at Ashridge Golf Club, where I was pro for some years. She loved life, did not train too much, but used to practise quite a bit. She had beautiful auburn hair, a freckled face and cheeky grin. The golfing public adored her. She was such a complete golfer that even when playing below form she was good enough to beat most of her contemporaries. She won both the American Ladies and the British Ladies titles in 1936.

Tragically, Pam was killed in a silly flying accident during the early days of the war when serving with the W.A.A.F. After a dance at a nearby Officers' Mess, her pilot boyfriend, who had borrowed a little training plane from their home air field, decided, in order not to fly over the Officers' Mess and risk an enquiry into what a plane was doing in the air at that time of the early morning, to push the plane onto the grass air field and take off downwind. Alas, the plane just failed to clear a building at the end of the field and they were both killed.

Doris Chambers

Pam Barton

Carrying Double

Carrying 'double' was no problem in the days when golf bags were small and light. The old local caddie at Ashridge Golf Club, where this photograph was taken in 1938, never refused to carry double; it was double money for an easy task. But to carry double today might mean humping more than 80lb. of dead weight over anything up to four and half miles and with five hours out there on the job!

I am wearing one of my Izod, heavy cashmere round-neck sweaters which never wore out; I gave them away.

Your right elbow can even float. Sevvy Balesteros really has a high right elbow.

Try some rounds with a No. 9 iron in your bag and no wedge, I bet you get better results on the average.

It doesn't matter what grip you use or how the hands lie on the club, the palms should be parallel to get a consistent result. Watch out for this.

Worth Knowing

This is a downhill chip shot from a scruffy lie and you can see that I play it with my right hand well down 'on the metal'. I play it with a hinged left wrist and from there, as I start on my way down, the hands will go forward so it will not be a lofted shot but a push onto the green with the hands low. This is the safest way to play it. Rest the right forearm on the right thigh, get well down to the ball, use a steep arc and then there is no risk of hitting too early and fluffing the shot. A timely nudge with the right knee adds authority to the stroke, but you need to practise.

Ditched at Penina

Here I am improvising a shot in order to show a pupil how I would handle a particularly awkward situation. With the ball in a ditch like this your backswing can't be measured, you can't use your hip action, and it is a challenge just to find the ball with the club head and make a true contact. The length you get depends entirely on the amount of flick you can impart with your wrists. There is no real alternative in this case. You have to go down on one knee to reach the ball, so you're dependent on your experience of the game and the feel you have for getting to the ball.

Not very long ago I found amongst my photographs this picture at Penina of the great American, Doug Sanders, playing a ditch shot from a very similar type of ditch although here he was able to get his foot down on the ditch bottom. He recovered well from this situation, I recall, because he has a particularly fine wrist and hand action. He also has a very wide stance for all his shots and probably the shortest backswing of any top class golfer I have known. He makes a very good and solid contact with the ball from even this most awkward stance and in this odd position his superb wrist technique enabled him to play out of trouble with complete confidence.

Doug Sanders

41

A Superb Stylist

Gene Littler is one of the game's supreme stylists and when you think of golfers playing with their knees sagging, body twisting as they go through the ball, and their heads sliding along with the club head, it's refreshing to see the ball hit in such a classical manner against the left leg and past the chin.

Gene has had trouble with cancerous growths under his left arm which were removed and which have weakened his left arm and hand, so he hits the ball more with the right now, no option. This picture was taken just before his major operation, but he's still playing many shots with both legs straight just a fraction after the impact. Study and learn from this action. You can still see the ball in flight, the club following on past his chin, and he's held the triangle formed by the shoulders and the grip absolutely perfectly. The club face has been brought square by an instinctive 'open to shut' roll. Few players have ever hit as many pure shots as Gene – the Machine.

Ben Crenshaw

Ben Crenshaw is one of the group of fine young American golfers who play great golf week after week and are all poised to hit the jackpot if they reach peak form in the right week. They play so many events that the very important U.S. Open is just another tournament. In my day The Open was *the* event – the real 'butterflies-in-the-tummy' test! When it was over – another year to wait.

Ben moves the top of his body from the ball in his backswing, but this is of no significance in his case because he finds the ball as well as anybody at impact and putts magnificently (and enjoys his superiority in this all-important part of the game). Curiously enough, he has a reputation amongst his colleagues of being a 'specialist trouble-shooter', a real 'three shots into two' artist!

Possibly the Greatest

If you did not know who the capped player was you would never believe he could be a real champ. He has just lifted the club straight up in the air, very little cock of the right wrist, club face fully open, back of the left hand in line with the forearm. Yet it is more than likely that this ball will be clouted 270 yards right down the middle of this huge practice ground. Because this is Jack Nicklaus's personal swing and he has done so well with it that it is not fair even to make a comment. But I do say this: it is one that very few can copy. He has also lifted the left heel quite considerably here, which should encourage people who are not succeeding with their feet flat on the ground throughout the swing to give this method a try. Jack says, 'I hit the ball very hard with my right hand.' So I am not entirely wrong when I advocate this in my teaching.

This other photograph shows a slim Jack Nicklaus on the first tee at Muirfield. He's certainly stayed behind that one and let it fly! From a wide stance too, and his left foot has slid round, almost to point to the target.

Hit the ball cleanly off the green – without scuffing the turf with the putter head. Most golfers do not. And remember that every putt is a straight putt: only the grain and the slope have to be studied.

I enjoy helping a golfer break 90 or 100 just as much and possibly even more than I enjoy helping a champion recover his form. The rabbit is often more grateful.

Do not be afraid to open the stance for big iron shots. Simply to pull the left foot back at address is often enough because the blade of the straight iron gets knocked open very easily on impact. Many long iron shots are sent to the right as the body braces and the hands lift. The hands can be kept lower if the heel of the right hand is allowed to ride on the left thumb, that is, slightly higher on the grip.

Tommy Armour, whose strength of hand was legendary, never ceased to emphasize that turning the body too fast, or letting the body do too much, was a major cause of slack iron shots. Like me he was a 'hands' man, and often said, 'Play with as little body interference as possible.'

Jacko!

Tony Jacklin a fraction before impact. A fine action photograph taken by Frank Gardner. Hands high, shaft in line with the left arm, tension stiff – so unlike the bent-arm action of Sevvy Ballesteros at this same point in the swing.

There is no doubt at all that Tony is hitting against his left side, with his left foot planted square to the line of flight. (I hate to disagree with so great a player as Tony, but I really cannot see the body doing 50 per cent of the work in this shot as he insists it is!)

44

A Stunning View

The picturesque Vale do Lobo course I designed on the Algarve had quite different construction problems from those of nearby Penina. The course lies on sand, partly in a fig orchard and partly in an umbrella pine forest. The challenge was not to take water off the land, but to bring water onto it; to cut out trees, not to plant them. I feel I can say I succeeded. This photograph shows me standing on the 7th tee, the start of a very pretty short hole running along the cliff-tops.

The Stroke Saver

A useful way of rolling three shots into two. From just off the green, in grass too thick to putt through, I'm using a No. 5 iron to 'throw' the ball onto a chosen spot on the green from where I reckon it will run forward to the hole for a simple putt.

Always look ahead. Play the shot that will make your next shot easy whenever you can. A superb hit is of no value if it leaves you with a difficult next shot.

When you win, everyone rushes to greet you. When you lose, you are on your own. That is a lesson every champion has had to learn – and has to live with.

You can chip the ball with the wrists stiff and push it, or use the wrists to flick it. Both work perfectly well, but make up your mind what you are going to do and do not mix the methods.

I like the quote by François Coppet saying, 'Who shall I imitate in order to be original?' I say to the young, 'Pick the bits of the action of successful older players you admire and see if they fit in your body.'

Missing a short putt does not mean you have to hit your next drive out of bounds.

You can learn to do a golf swing without a ball but you cannot learn to strike a ball without training the muscles to absorb the shock of impact.

Too many golfers stand too near the ball, before and after they hit it. I said it first.

It is characteristic of Cotton to take things hard, whether the playing of the game, the whispering of the crowd, or the legislation of the authorities, but these qualities, if they make for suffering, also make for greatness, and here is a very great and originally minded golfer . . .
BERNARD DARWIN

Joe Carr

The Firm Left Side

A cartoonist's impression of me aged twenty-one, showing a firm left side and one of my favourite fair isle sweaters! I have always hit against a firm left side. A young Gary Player did too, and so did Joe Carr from Dublin, Eire.

GARY PLAYER'S GOLF CLASS:

Plant that left foot

YOUR LEFT FOOT IS *SWIVELLING* ROUND AS YOU HIT THROUGH THE BALL, TOM

WHEN YOUR FOOT TURNS, YOU ARE NOT THEN HITTING UP AGAINST A *FIRM LEFT SIDE*. ALSO, YOUR CLUB GOES THROUGH TO THE *LEFT* INSTEAD OF STRAIGHT TO THE TARGET

MIKE SOUCHAK USED TO HAVE A LOT OF TROUBLE WITH THIS AND SO DID I. I CURED MYSELF ON THE PRACTICE TEE BY HAMMERING A TENT PEG INTO THE GROUND, WHICH KEPT MY FOOT FROM TURNING

HENRY COTTON HAD THE BEST LEFT FOOT POSITION I EVER SAW – HE KEPT IT *PLANTED* JUST PERFECTLY!

STRAIGHT

LEFT

TENT PEG →

© BEAVERBROOK NEWSPAPERS LTD. 1970

46

Cotton was sustained, in many ways, by the wealthy
and highly perceptive Argentinian who became his wife.
He and his friends called her Toots. It is arguable
whether he could have achieved what he did without her
LADDIE LUCAS

Gary Player

Toots

The first moment I ever set eyes on the woman
who was to have the greatest influence on my
life. She was snapped by the club photographer
of the Mar del Plata Golf Club, the most
popular seaside golf club in Argentina, in
January 1930. Arriving at the club for her first
lesson, we met about ten seconds after this
picture was taken. She had booked fifty lessons
without ever seeing me! I found the photo on the
club notice board where the photographer invited
orders from those he had snapped. I bought it!

A player may, without penalty, place his clubs
in a hazard prior to making a stroke provided
nothing is done which may improve the lie of
the ball or constitute testing the soil.

If you use a reverse hand putting grip, index
finger of the left hand over the right hand little
finger, remember it will also work well for little
shots around the green with any club.

Some of our young professionals forget that
even if they consider themselves 'small stars',
there is no need to 'take' all the time, they
must give as well. You can accept hospitality
but you have an obligation to return some too.

My Golfer

The year is 1930 and here is my new pupil from the Argentine. I am coaching her with hickory-shafted clubs and from this moment on we became very great friends. Eventually I got her to play quite decently, mainly by telling her she was no good, had no chance, and so on. (I think this is the only way to tell any woman to do something you want her to do – tell her she can't. It still works fifty years later!)

In the end she became quite a good little player with an 8 handicap and won the Austrian Ladies Open Championship in 1937. We married in 1939 and here I am in R.A.F. uniform, double Open Champion, being used as a porter by my wife, Toots, on her way to compete in a war charity event just after the war had started. On

A Really Solid Striker

Sam Snead, that great swinger of the club (perhaps the greatest ever) has the most remarkable arms and hands. He has double-jointed wrists, which helps him tremendously, and is so strong that he used to do one-handed press-ups as though he weighed five stone rather than thirteen. When you are trying to compare yourself with Sam just bear this in mind.

Snead goes from his beautiful top-of-the-swing position, perfectly balanced, to a finish which is equally controlled and well poised. This 'posing' is preached by many teachers as the secret of golf, though to me it has always been the part from 9 o'clock to 3 o'clock that counts. Even for Sam, with that lovely swing, there was no guarantee that he was going to make a perfect impact, *unless* he guided the club face to the centre of the back of the ball and this he has been doing instinctively ever since he was a kid.

I have known Sam from his early twenties and have been a great admirer of both his golf and the way he has handled his career. He has made a lot of money and has done it really on his own. He has not been pushed along by anybody, he has just paddled his own canoe, and now it is so full of gold it can hardly stay afloat!

that occasion she was partnered by the late Mrs Frances 'Bunty' Stephens, that frail little golfer with one of the longest pauses at the top I have seen in major golf. Toots, I recall, did not disgrace herself that day, playing in such famous company.

Her first clubs were short 'ladies-weight' ones, as I was taught suited most women, and she did reasonably well with them. Then one day she was watching me practise and picked up one of my clubs and hit a ball with it. It went twenty yards further. 'Oh!' was the reaction. 'So you didn't want me to improve, I can see.' Was I embarrassed? It took me years to live this down. All husbands can see themselves in my shoes!

It Is Tiring

As the human being is not a machine, it rests finally on the fingers to guide the club face squarely to the ball. Any change in the final pressure can affect the hand action and so alter both the club face impact position and the timing. Difficulties with the golf swing arise from the fact that the left-arm blow is back-handed, whilst the right-hand blow is fore-handed, and so whatever the type of grip of the club employed, it must be taken to enable the hands to deliver the blow when working together to the best advantage.

How many people play golf today with their hands so badly placed on the shaft that if the hands were to be used individually they simply could not deliver a decent whack at the ball? Millions, one can safely say. Believe me, if your hands, used independently, cannot send a golf ball somewhere towards the target you are not

going to use them properly together.

The shape of the hands themselves guides golfers into the type of grip they use best, and the volumes written on where to grip, with which fingers, and where the shaft should lie in the hands, amount to nothing more than individual golfers describing how *they* do it best.

'Now grip the club as if you were about to shake hands, about as tightly as you grip your knife and fork.' 'Grip firmly with the index finger and thumb of both hands.' 'Grip with the last two fingers of the left hand.' 'Use a long thumb' (that is, with the thumb extended down the shaft as far as possible). All such tips, valuable as they can be for certain people, aid only temporarily. The basic need for control of the tension by individual fingers of both hands still exists for all.

Grip thickness plays a considerable part in this

tension control, yet few golfers today ever experiment; they buy a set of clubs and mould their game around the clubs, being satisfied with whatever thickness of grip the club maker has fitted. However, it is obvious that with thinner grips the club shafts lie more in the fingers and this encourages lively wrist action and a freer stroke, whilst the thicker grip, as can readily be felt if a tennis racquet is gripped as if it were a golf shaft, chokes the hands and seems to tighten or block the wrists.

This control of the grip tension means not freezing on to the shaft like a man clinging to a life-raft but being able to work up to the correct tension so as not to tire the grip during the swing, which causes a player to let go at impact, or grip too tightly and slow up the wrist action.

I am not one of those who thinks the only way to play golf is to close the fingers of both hands firmly on the shaft so that the shaft and arms are all one and must remain so throughout the swing. I am with the school which claims that the club must only be held tightly enough to stop it turning in the hands during a full stroke, and that if the strength of the fingers is built up, then up to five consecutive full shots can be played without having to adjust the fingers on the shaft. This I put as a sort of passing-out test to my students. There is a world of difference between a 'piccolo player', one who opens one or both hands during the swing and allows a twist, and a player with a solid, vice-like grip.

There is no need to do a drag back of the hands as exaggerated as I am doing in the photograph, but it does get rid of a lot of tension in the take-away – it helps to flail. Just how relaxed the grip can afford to be depends on the wrists and hands of the individual player.

The Par-dré

Here I am with Father Len Scannell, a Catholic priest from America, who was an assistant golf pro before he went into the priesthood and then he joined the American Air Force as a chaplain, where he worked until he retired.

The story of Father Len is really quite unusual because he loved golf so much that every hour he had free he used to play. He loved competing and enjoyed Pro-Ams and Invitational events. Whenever an aeroplane was doing a duty run he would try and get a lift from his base and appear in a Pro-Am somewhere, usually playing so well that his name began to appear too frequently in the list of winners. This was noticed by Catholic authorities in the American Air Force, so he adopted the 'noms de plume' of O'Connell, O'Donnell and O'Brien! He was posted at one period to Alaska, which was a pretty rough move for a golfing enthusiast, but even so he managed to get the odd trip by freight plane down to the States to play golf. Everybody loves him; he is nicknamed 'The Par-dré'.

I met him first in America on one of my early trips there and afterwards he came over to Britain where this picture was taken outside local pro Eddie Musty's tent at Royal Lytham and St Anne's during the Ryder Cup matches.

Father Len eventually retired from the American Air Force and, in his search for a post where he could play golf, he ended up as a curate in Northern California, only to find that his boss there also played golf and there wasn't enough time for them both to get off and play at the same time. He is now in Palm Springs in California as a curate where he can play more golf as his boss is not a golfer. Every afternoon you can find him out somewhere in the desert, where there are twenty courses, making the odd dollar. He is over seventy years of age and can still shoot in the seventies. A great guy!

What Are the Odds?

Now for one of those 'believe-it-or-not' stories. I was invited to play at Temple Golf Club with some friends: (left to right) Tim Glover of Lloyds, Peter Nelson the race-horse trainer, Pat Milligan of Lloyds, and Charles Hughesdon, a non-golfer, one of the big insurance brokers in the City. We stopped just by the short 13th and were photographed. At that moment the conversation curiously had drifted on to the odds on a 'hole in one' and these gentlemen from Lloyds, no strangers to the business of risk-taking, asked me, 'What really are the odds against a hole in one?'

They had often covered this risk at golf tournaments and even at some exhibition games, but I told them that I couldn't give an exact figure for the odds because it depended on the quality of the players and the number of shots taken by each. In a recent American experiment, the local pro had tried one particular 148-yard hole at his club and it took him 4,580 shots to make an 'ace'. And that was several days' shooting by a man who knew the length and lie of the hole and had played it countless times. Any player familiar with a course must have a better chance of a hole in one than a player new to the course, but even then, and excluding the professionals, I guessed the odds must be about ten thousand to one against on one selected hole, but if the bet was for an ace anywhere on the course, usually four short holes, then say six thousand to one.

The 13th at Temple is a short hole of 150 yards on rising ground which hides the bottom of the flag from the tee. It was my honour and we were still discussing this business of the odds when I played – I hit the ball straight into the hole before their very eyes! In a long golfing career I have hit eighteen aces but never one so perfectly timed.

Kel Nagle

A good action shot of that great Australian golfer Kel Nagle playing his second to the 16th green at St Andrews on his way to win the Centenary Open in 1960. Nagle came to Britain in the late forties. Initially he made little impact on the golfing scene, then suddenly, a decade later, he became a golfing machine. He is a very strong fellow with a tightly controlled swing and he addresses the ball in a unique way – with the club head a head's length on the inside of the ball. Then he 'stretches out' on the way through, playing with very simple footwork and practically no hip action, and still hits the ball very solidly indeed. Though shortening his swing lost him some yards from the tee from his early professional days when he really flogged it a long way, this simplifying of his golf game led him to fame and wealth. But his putting, using a firm arm stroke with virtually no wrist action, really carried him through to his place in the history of golf.

Kel Nagle on his way to winning the
Centenary Open, St Andrews, 1960

A Great Competitor

Michael Bonallack was one of the great amateur golfers of postwar years, a marvellous competitor whose record included five amateur championships. In this first picture he is hitting almost as late as it's possible to hit. His hands are down almost to his knees and it looks physically impossible for him to bring the club into the ball at all, let alone squarely. I took the photograph while watching him practise at Temple Golf Club. At that time he was trying to limit a tendency to fade more than he liked, although it did not cost him very much, as he knew it was coming, and he was always prepared to allow for it. This, and his sensational putting, were enough to handle most of the problems he came across on the golf course.

I think this second picture of Michael, well after impact, helps to explain his rare golfing ability. He's managed to find the ball by coming up on the toes of both feet, and that, of course, is correct and instinctive. It is, in fact, very common, particularly in tall golfers who have to crouch at address, hit late and very hard. They are inclined to compensate for the risk of hitting the ground behind the ball by raising the whole of the swing.

Weak Knees

Competitors in the Portuguese Open at Penina some years back, snapped by my camera, driving off the first tee. This is their interpretation of the modern action, young fellows using their knees and body to propel the golf ball. My serious comment? Whenever I see anybody produce that swing as 'the latest and the most powerful action in golf' I feel I want to guffaw like a donkey. Because to me that is a weak-kneed and slack position, and even if they do hit well at times it must be one of the most difficult positions from which to strike a golf ball solidly. The legs are acting as a sort of jelly layer underneath the body and I do not think anyone could hit ten good shots in succession with that sort of action. If I told these golfers to do the direct opposite of what they have in mind, they could probably hit the ball 100 per cent better.

The Age to Begin

Here is a young lad, eleven years of age at the time, knocking balls into a net in the garden of the family home on the fifteenth fairway of the Burma Road course at Wentworth, Surrey. He was really 'having a go' and I thought then that he would get somewhere because he was not afraid to attack the golf ball and he seemed to be able to hold the club well, as you can see here. He has a good right hand position, and I was giving him an idea of how to start the club back, just to turn round himself, and he seemed to do it very easily. The boy, son of Brigadier A. C. Critchley and his second wife Diana Fishwick, is Bruce Critchley, later to become a Walker Cup player. You really cannot start golf too young. I suppose the deciding factor is the child's ability to concentrate on what he is doing, not so much his age.

Smart Smith

Macdonald Smith, one of the famous Smith brothers from Carnoustie, Scotland, who went to America to win fame and fortune. Mac was probably the best of the whole family as a player, but his brother Alex won the U.S. Open. He had a beautiful slow rhythm, and he had the extraordinary habit of actually stopping at the top of his backswing for every stroke. I took this shot at the top of the backswing for a putt, where he naturally paused, and from there he hit the ball beautifully and smoothly.

It is a great test of nerves to be able to do this at all. He pointed his left elbow to the hole and had his right thumbnail stuck into the grip of his club. I have seen this done before but the combination of all plus a pause, never. I do not know whether or not he eventually developed a twitch, but this is certainly a good way to acquire one!

Mac was always a natty dresser – note his striped shirt, bow tie, and two-tone shoes.

It Did Happen!

Now this gentleman, discussing his grip with me, came into my life when I was consultant and golf advisor at the Mougins Golf Club near Cannes, France, back in the sixties. I received a telephone call from Vancouver Island, Canada, from a Mr Percy Widdup, to ask if he could come and spend six weeks with me in Cannes. I said, 'Of course,' and so began a long friendship.

I found out that he was a golf nut and that he had consulted at least thirty other pros in Canada and America about his golf game. He played to a 6 handicap and couldn't understand why he was unable to get it lower. I began to work with him and found that he allowed the club to slip in his hands for all his shots. It didn't matter how he corrected the position of his grip at address; by the time he had hit the ball he had always reverted to a four-knuckle grip, right hand under the shaft, so the club face was not always square enough to make a regular solid impact. Like many people with this type of fault he did not want to *know* that the club was slipping. He hoped for a tip to cure his problem, i.e. a quick cure. I didn't think he was prepared to do a lot of work to correct this slip because he had been doing it for so long. So I suggested that he should not use a driver (which is no disgrace – Peter Thomson won all his Opens driving with a lofted wooden club). But in his heart Percy wanted to drive with a driver and he wouldn't settle for anything else. He was a splendid person and over the years became a very good friend. But you can't have a winner every time. Not every violinist, even if he practised twenty-four hours a day, could become another Menuhin. Unless you have real talent there is no chance of becoming even a very good golfer. You can be a decent player, but to be very good is a gift given to very few people.

Percy Widdup really was quite a character and perhaps the most memorable thing about him was the incredible story he told me about his experiences during, and just after, the war. It seems that before the war Percy had a successful business in the Far East, selling and repairing farm machinery, trucks and tractors, which enabled him to live a very comfortable life and play golf to his heart's content. But early in the war the area was taken over by the Japanese and Percy was captured. As he could speak a number

of the local dialects he was made spokesman for the prisoners of the camp in which he was incarcerated somewhere near Singapore. Percy managed to survive the war and finally the day came when he was released. He made his way back to the area in which his factory was located and asked a taxi driver to drop him within half a mile of the plant so that he could walk along to it and see if there were any changes, or even if it was still there. The nearer he got, the more puzzled he became. It all looked so different. And there, on what he calculated was his site, was a building he had never seen before, an enormous building with a wire fence all round it and a guard on the gate. There was no name, no sign, but he knew this must be the place. He asked the man at the gate if this was the site of the Widdup plant and was told, 'Yes sir, please go straight in.' He walked through beautifully kept gardens and into the entrance hall of the building where twin staircases led up to a gallery. 'It must be the main office,' he thought, but still he saw nobody. At last he pushed open an impressive door and there was a beautiful office, tastefully furnished, a big desk, fitted carpets, matching curtains, and a fireplace, and over the fireplace a painting of himself!

And then, he said, he cried like a child. He didn't know if he was dreaming or if it was true, but there it was; there was his portrait and there was his own huge desk, with telephones and intercoms. He went to one of the adjoining rooms and came face to face with his two former partners both of them Chinese. When Percy had walked out with his captors years before he had had no opportunity to take anything, no chance to leave any instructions. He just left, thinking he would never return. Now the three of them were able to exchange stories of what had happened to them.

His partners had been able and willing to carry on the business throughout the war years. They had managed to keep the team together and emerge not only still in business but highly successful. So much so that they had completely rebuilt the factory. Moreover, behind the walls of the upstairs offices were secret safes full of money, even some gold bars. They took Percy to the safes, handed him the keys, said it was all his and bowed themselves out.

It was a long time before Percy was able to pull himself together. He hadn't thought such people existed. For years they had not known where he was, whether or not he was alive even. And he had walked out of internment straight into a fortune. Finally he decided to retire to Canada, leaving the business to the remarkable men who had held it in trust for him for so many years.

Less Turn

U.S. master golfer Ray Floyd seen driving at Royal Birkdale. Ray has very long legs for his height and his trunk is comparatively short. Here he is using what I think is a narrow stance for him. He is hitting this ball mainly with his hands because he has not allowed much of a hip or shoulder turn.

Ray uses a mallet type putter made $2\frac{1}{2}$ inches longer than standard, which means he can stand very upright for his putts; this means practice on the green is not a back-tiring job.

He is some putter.

Tony Jacklin

In 1963 Tony Jacklin won my Rookie award for the best young player in that year, and here he is with me holding his prize cheque, which I still present annually to be best young pro in his first year in competition. Who would have thought that six years later this boy would be acknowledged one of the greats of all time! For after winning The Open at Royal Lytham in 1969 he won the American Open the following June in 1970, and so for a brief month he held both titles – a really tremendous feat.

The picture of a young Tony was taken at his peak. He is in full control of his swing. He has

started the 'pull down', as you can see from the bend in the shaft. The club face is almost fully open, and he is well balanced on both feet ready to lash the ball. Jack Nicklaus liked Jacklin's swing at this period; his hands were under the shaft and he had no tension in his hands, wrists and forearms then. Often some tension can be observed now.

Tony liked riding on Pacifico, my sweet old donkey. When he was still the American Open Champion he came to Penina for a holiday. He had just lost his British title to Jack Nicklaus at St Andrews where he went to the turn in a

fabulous 29 in one round, only to have his round interrupted by a violent storm which flooded the course. Play was resumed the following day.

He loved Penina and enjoyed swimming in the huge Olympic-size pool there. That was the only thing that I didn't approve of. I have always believed that swimming is bad for a golfer, but he continued to enjoy it and that was his business. We played golf together every day during his visit. He still played well, but the edge had gone; he'd relaxed, he'd had enough golf, he'd made a lot of money, and enjoyed two weeks getting away from it all.

What has happened to him since? Well, everybody has his or her own theory. He's still the same fellow. He's made some money, he has an elegant home in Jersey, a lovely family and a beautiful wife, so maybe it is fulfilment of so many ambitions that is responsible for his mediocre success in the past few years. In 1979 there was a sort of comeback, some high finishes and two major title wins, so there is still a possibility he could be regaining that missing something in his golf life, which we would all like to see.

Gary Player's Hook

'How can you be right and everyone else wrong?' said Gary Player to me some years ago when he was hooking every fifth or sixth full shot and I told him to use his right hand more. On a narrow course, or if the hook happened to come on the wrong hole on a reasonably open course, it put him right out of contention. It was almost like the torture of a player expecting a shank at any moment, every day!

He had been troubled with this problem for some time and what prompted him to utter the words was that he had been seeking to cure this damaging hook by making his left arm and side do more in his swing, cutting out his right hand altogether, as is classically accepted. Said one teaching pro, 'You are surely not clearing your left side Gary. I'll fix you.' I told Gary discreetly after I had heard this, 'That is *not* right. I'll be at the back of the crowd when you practise tomorrow and if the hook still happens I'll come and whisper to you what to do.' You can just see me at the back of the crowd in the photograph, just after I had told Gary to hold his left heel up and to kill the ball with his right hand, the very *opposite* of what he was trying to do. Holding the left heel up blocks the left side and *makes* the right hand work.

Here the little wizard is trying it out. It worked. He was amazed. 'Are you there Mr Cotton?' After seeing him hit the ball harder and harder and straighter and straighter with his very powerful right hand I came forward again and

GARY PLAYER'S GOLF CLASS

Improve your hand action

I'M *PUSHING* EVERYTHING OUT TO THE *RIGHT*, GARY!

YOU *CERTAINLY* ARE, IAIN. YOUR *HAND ACTION* IS ABSOLUTELY *DEAD*

IF YOU REALLY WANT TO FEEL YOUR HANDS WHIP THROUGH THE BALL, GO ONTO THE PRACTICE AREA AND HIT A FEW BALLS KEEPING YOUR *LEFT HEEL RAISED OFF THE GROUND*

© BEAVERBROOK NEWSPAPERS LTD. 1978

HENRY COTTON GAVE ME THIS TIP DURING THE *1971 DUNLOP MASTERS TOURNAMENT* IN *WALES*. I ACTUALLY PLAYED THE FINAL ROUND KEEPING MY HEEL UP *THROUGHOUT* THE SWING, AND I SHOT *66!*

Script by Iain Reid, Drawings by Gary Keane from photographs by Sidney Harris.

Golfers can be great bores . . . I developed a remarkable instinct in the detection of bores at first sight . . . But
with Cotton I could stay up all night talking golf
HENRY LONGHURST

said, 'Fade the ball now.' 'I have never power-
faded a ball in my life,' he said. 'How?' 'Play it
by instinct. Just work the club face across the
ball slightly with your right hand,' I said. All this
in a whisper. Not a soul heard what we said.

The result was that the ball drifted steadily to
the right and the caddie had to go even further
back as the slight breeze was from behind and
from the left.

Gary was scared to use this 'gimmick' right
away but finally, after a few expensive hooks
returned in the opening rounds of the 1971
Dunlop Masters at St Pierre C.C., Chepstow,
where he played the final round – in 66 – with
his heel up throughout. 'Could have been a 60!'
said Gary. 'I knocked the sticks out.'

The following week he beat Jack Nicklaus by
five' and four in the final of the Piccadilly World
Matchplay Tournament at Wentworth – still with
his heel up. But I warned him then, 'Don't stick
to the heel up technique for too long. Drop it as
soon as you begin to use the right hand properly
– as you always do, for example, for your
fabulous bunker play.' 'Yes,' he answered
thoughtfully, 'I am all right-handed from the
sand.'

This 'left heel up' tip works well for most
errors in golf where the hands are not working
correctly, as referred to in Gary's Golf Class
strip, where the heel can be up to get a square
hit for someone going to the right too. A
valuable 'square strike' tip!

I dislike looking for golf balls unless it is for my
opponents in a needle match, but I never get
the watch out and never have, as I would hate
getting a hole this way, but I lost one once in
the 1921 Boys Championship.

I hate a dirty ball, equally I like a new shiny
one, especially when it goes off with a lovely
click on impact.

I cannot bear to hit a soft, no-sound ball; it
feels to me like playing with the club head cover
on.

Respect age – it does not look well to be
familiar when you first meet a senior person.
Wait till you are made to feel it is right before
you are fresh. You gain by being correct.

Henry Longhurst

I knew Henry Longhurst well. In fact, we spoke
on the phone not many hours before he died. I
think I first met him when he was a member of
the Cambridge University Golf Team in the
1930s.

My picture shows him in 1949, just back from
army service and picking up the threads of his
fabulous writing career, which had been
interrupted by the war. I rather like that cheeky
smirk on his face. He had a great sense of
humour which we both understood, which is why
we got on so well. He could play scratch golf but
used to hit the ball with an unwanted slice. He
used to call it the 'Bedfordshire Fade' because at
his home club in Bedford there was 'out of
bounds' all round the course on the left. The
holes ran clockwise round the course and he was
scared to lose his ball if he hit it left. This
encouraged the beginnings of a slice that was to
haunt him for years. He never fully corrected it.

He really enjoyed his golf, and liked
competition, but when that dreaded 'twitch' on
the green appeared he put his clubs in the attic
for good. He was one of the first people to
'boast' of having a twitch, but from being a joke
it actually became a tragedy. He tried to beat it
and take the club back on short putts in all
different ways, but when he tried to take it
forward the putter head flew at the ball like a
terrier at a rat, and at all sorts of angles. This
was *more* than he could stand.

On Dave Thomas

There was a time when David Thomas was one of the longest and straightest drivers in the history of the game. He tied for The Open in 1958 and lost the play-off. He was also runner-up again in 1966. I think he was very unlucky not to win in 1958. He went through the back of the 71st green at Royal Lytham with a glorious second shot: the ball rolled over the top of a little bank behind the green, and it couldn't have been more than five yards from the flag. Down in two would have put him in the clear lead. But the short pitch was a shot he couldn't play. The grass was a bit thick, he couldn't really take his putter to it as he used to do for safety when he could and so he chipped it – jerkily as usual – and finished well short of the hole. Dave missed the putt, finished in a tie, and then lost on the play-off to Peter Thomson.

I have known David Thomas since he was a very young man and he had a fabulous gift, he could go through the ball in one piece with his driver and hit it miles absolutely squarely, and on the upswing, using a high peg. He was a wonderful tee shot player, and one winter he and Guy Wolstenholme, both giants came to Mougins Golf Club, behind Cannes in the South of France, to train at the course where Toots and I played regularly. We played together for a whole month. I had already finished competitive golf and Dave was just in his prime, but the odd thing was that on that course, which was on the short side, he rarely beat me. This was largely because he could be counted on now and then to hit a shot thirty yards or so over a green and into the jungle or out of bounds and lose a hole that he could reach with a driver and a lofted iron while I was often taking two big shots to get on. It was so ridiculous that I began to query whether he could really see well. So I said to him on one round, 'Can you read the numbers on that tee box?' He nearly said, 'What box?' so I asked him to shut one eye, then the other eye, and he said, 'Yes, with one eye I can just about read it. But with the other eye I can't see anything, the box looks a blur.'

We finished that round and the next morning

on the way to the golf course I took him to a
local optician. He wasn't an eye specialist but he
tried him with some of those test glasses, doing
the usual changes of lenses, and found that
David had one eye which wasn't very good, but
could be helped with a suitable lens, while the
other was more or less O.K. So in a couple of
days Dave had a pair of spectacles which he
hadn't realized he needed. From the moment on
he judged the ball much better. But his main
golfing problem remained: he simply could not
pitch the ball. If you gave him a good lie and a
shot from forty yards or less to a green, he
would make an awful mess of it. If the ball was
lying badly, in a divot mark for instance, as it
was when he played the shot in the photograph,
he handled it perfectly. The problem remained
throughout his career. I tried to help, every other
player, friend and coach tried, but we never
achieved any lasting success in making Dave play
this length of pitch shot well. Now he has wisely
given up tournaments and is a successful golf
architect.

The Golden Boy

The grooved and very personal short backswing
of Bernard 'Big Ben' Hunt was a model of
control and economy of movement. He had a
very calm disposition, ideal for golf. His swing
was controlled, his temper was controlled, and he
just hit shot after shot with one of the most
precise and economical and brief actions of
modern times.

One of the stories told about Bernard Hunt is
that during a match lightning flashed somewhere
quite near him and from the shock he dropped
his club. When somebody asked him what
happened he said, 'Oh, I got my four all right.'
He is a superb putter who meticulously kept his
brass-headed centre-shafted club in a leather
cover, and still does. With his golden hair and
amazing run of successes he was dubbed 'The
Golden Boy' when he came onto the golf scene
and began to win in the big tournaments. He had
a long spell collecting first prize cheques and then
got out in time to enjoy teaching the game and
living a less strenuous life.

Trick-Shot Man

THE CLUB PRO GOES HIKING

Joe Kirkwood was always good for a laugh, even with his Christmas cards. He sent me this one years ago. He was also the original, and perhaps the greatest, trick-shot artist of them all. He performed without the aid of a microphone no matter what the size of the crowd and entertained with a unique blend of marvellous technical skill and pure slapstick comedy.

One of his favourite, and most popular, tricks started with him asking if anyone in the crowd could kindly lend him a pocket watch. Very reluctantly one would be produced. It might, for example, be a gold presentation watch. Joe would assure the anxious owner that there was no danger, he was quite proficient at the trick. 'Sir! There is really no risk!' he would say, palming the watch expertly and replacing it with a cheap subsitute without anyone seeing. Then he would put the watch on the ground, very carefully tee up a ball on a piece of plasticine on the glass face of the watch, and do some practice swings, very near the watch, with a wooden club. He would take the most enormous divots out of the tee as he warmed up for his trick, and everybody would roar with laughter at the obvious discomfort of the owner of the watch. 'Don't be nervous, Sir,' he would say, 'this is a trick I never miss. I've done it a thousand times. And an even bigger divot would fly through the air. 'Never mind, when it comes to the trick I always pull myself together,' and with this he would address the ball, hesitate a few times, then give an almighty slash, hitting watch, golf ball, the whole lot out of sight. Once the laughter had subsided he would finally put the owner out of his misery and return his watch to him.

With Joe Kirkwood

In a round of golf if you used, say, a No. 7 every time you had an open shot to the green of fifty yards or under with no intervening trap to the pin, you would save shots; try it and see.

On the way out is the belief that softer golf balls, that is lower compression balls, suit weaker golfers. Now the pundits have discovered that the tighter and harder ball is best for everyone.

If you have a poor grip and you know it, you can train your hands to hold the club correctly much more easily by working out on a tyre than by hitting golf balls, believe me.

Leonard Crawley

I first met Leonard Crawley, that great all-round sportman, long before he became a golf journalist. He was a scratch golfer and also played county cricket for Essex. He was an opening bat and treated every ball on its merits. If the first ball was not a good one there was no question of waiting to get his eye in – he would send it to the boundary. Leonard was an outstanding games player, and golf came most naturally to him. He once played in the first winning Walker Cup side and later wrote on golf for the *Daily Telegraph* for many, many years. After the match, he went and hit 118 runs before lunch as an opener for Essex v. Glamorgan. He said I had trained his hands so well cricket was easy. It was his last county game.

He had a great sense of humour. Here he is with a cowboy stetson, which he always wore at 'The Masters' in Augusta, Georgia. His clothing was outrageous. He used to wear ginger woollen plus four suits; it was said he was colour blind.

He never forgot that I taught him a two-knuckle grip when he came to Belgium for a week's tuition in the thirties. He knew his four-knuckle grip was letting him down and he liked my consistent striking with a two-knuckle grip and a relaxed left arm at address. He succeeded in playing his scratch golf or better, with a unique slow backswing action, which was very rhythmical, and inspiring to watch. His putting was suspect, which I believe was responsible for him not cleaning up in the amateur world.

Practising with
Ben Hogan

Tournament golfers have a bond and so I got to know Ben Hogan well, or as well as any man could, for he never was an easy man to know. He has a few friends, whom he likes and understands and who understand him, but otherwise he is a loner. I found him a fascinating character. He dedicated himself to golf and became a wonderful player.

When I took this picture of him playing in

1947, he was using a method which, after his accident, he discarded. As you can see, he is driving with a very lofted wood – a lofted No. 2 – with which he hit the ball quite a long way with a big draw. His weakness was that like all people playing with a four-knuckle grip, he at times let the club move in his hands and hooked badly. As I got to know him better we practised together quite a lot and strangely he could not play a half shot at that time because his left arm tended to collapse and the hook could be unbelievable. Later he suffered his awful car crash, and spent many months afterwards trying to get his legs right. He trained his hands on a trapeze over the bed, and when he came to play again he had his greatest years – even with a power-fade at one stage. What a marvellous competitor! He had great concentration and he understood his own game perfectly. He never liked teaching, and gave few lessons, but he certainly enjoyed spending hours on the practice ground and still does.

The group photograph shows Ben Hogan as Captain of the U.S. Ryder Cup Team in Portland, Oregon, 1947. This was the year we got thrashed; not too surprising as we travelled to America by ship and then travelled almost five days by train 3,000 miles across the American continent. We played the British-made large ball, which was not a very good one at that time, and on a course we never really saw, as it was practically under water, and after being there seven days we still had not practised properly. Robert Hudson, who was the host for both teams, asked if we would please play the match. It was costing him many thousands of dollars a day and the weather forecast was endless rain. We agreed and got badly beaten. I did enquire, as I kept up my friendship with Bob, 'When did the rain finally stop?' It was thirty days later, so we did Bob a good turn. He remained a friend of the British Ryder Cup players of that year, and many other home players, right up until his death, which came at a period when he had lost his fortune.

The Greatest Aussie

Peter Thomson came into golf shortly after I had retired from the tournament game, but it was very easy to see that this young Australian, then just twenty-one years of age, was a very mature person. The Aussies seem to bloom early and he brought to golf another picture, another image. He was smiling, he gave the impression of enjoying his golf, and of being casual. In fact it was an act, for he had a calculating brain far beyond his years. I never saw him pace out any shots when he first arrived in Great Britain. He just walked briskly up to the ball and played his shot. He had a regular caddie (who you can see in the picture) who was a good friend and guide to him, but he decided every shot himself.

An unusual feature of Peter's play was that he allowed the club to slip in his grip in all his shots. He never worried about the club moving in his hands, in fact he thought it was quite normal, while I had always been brought up to dread the club moving even a little. Today, one of the tests I give my young players is to check, when they have finished a shot, whether the club has moved at all, but Peter Thomson and Neil Coles are two superb players who actually allow the club to twist in their hands. Oddly, they are both very accurate players, which debunks in a way my belief that you have to hold on very solidly all the time. I have talked with both of them about this point and neither can play golf any other way. Nor can Dai Rees, another very consistent (and now veteran) golfer, who always allows his right-hand grip to slip but maintains a firm left-hand grip throughout his stroke.

Thomson is also interesting for the fact that he always lets his head go with the ball; he's never tried to hit past his chin because he found it blocked him in some way. In this shot you can see he's played with the club face held slightly down. He's hammered the ball a bit and his right shoulder is well under, but his head is turned with his follow-through. Perhaps not text-book golf – but his record stands up to any in the world magnificently. Some people have faulted him for not having won in America, but he played there very little. I think that one of life's privileges is to be free to go and play where one likes and when one likes. To have to go and do a certain thing, just to prove something, may satisfy some critics but I certainly don't regard

Thomson as a poorer player because he didn't like competing in America. Nor is it fair to criticize someone like Neil Coles because he doesn't like flying – a conviction that cuts out much of the joy of going to America because it is such a long journey by ship. The travel factor is something to bear in mind when comparing past and present golfers. For Hagen and Jones, for example, each major overseas event took more or less a month out of their lives by the time they had left America and returned. Now, a competitor can play a tournament in America one week and be in Japan the next – feeling fit and relaxed, with no loss of form and with no losing of sea legs to worry about.

Another feature of Peter Thomson's casual game is his habit of allowing his left arm to bend quite freely and his left shoulder to point at the ball at the top of the backswing. The club face shut, or half shut, in his case depends on what shot he is going to play. He stands more or less flat-footed, raises the club almost to the height of his head, and strikes the ball without worrying about a big extension of both arms. He always has driven very straight, often with a lofted club because he hammered the ball down a bit and his down swing was therefore steep, almost the same as for an iron shot. He was always going to miss a few greens, he felt, for he was going to hit the odd poor shot, but he putted well instinctively and somehow he thought it was a simple part of the game for him. Peter was one of the greatest 'holers out' we ever had in golf, because I think his nerve and confidence were so good, he never allowed himself to worry about missing one now and then.

> Golfers who tend to strike too early can cure themselves of the habit by pretending to cut the ball with their hands as they go through the impact area. This usually produces a dead straight shot or even a slight draw because all that happens is that the left arm works perfectly and does not become a partner in an attempt to produce a wide artificial follow-through.
>
> There was a moment in golf history when a set of golf clubs could have been ten clubs, not fourteen, which perhaps would have been better, who knows?

An Unusual Grip

The top of the backswing for a No. 8 iron shot by Kel Nagle in his greatest year, 1960. What is interesting here is the odd position of the index finger of the right hand. It is not overlapping, it is just pushed in between the first and the second fingers of his left hand. I do not recall having tried this, though I must have done it some time in my life for I have tried almost everything. But I cannot recall any particular advantage or disadvantage. However, for those who experiment, there it is.

From this top of the swing position Nagle will squeeze the ball, taking a shallow divot, very straight, as can be noted from the divot marks ahead of his ball. It is always interesting to note how players, when hitting a series of balls, tear off turf from a huge area.

I remember years ago watching that ardent practicer Frank 'Muscles' Stranahan strip a very large area of turf – it took him three hours! Naturally I was not there all the time, I had played eighteen holes meantime, but on passing to and from my car I saw him hard at it. Far too long a spell, for he would be working out with tiring muscles.

A First Look at the Proette Circus
Nancy Lopez

It is impossible to keep up to date with golf news, things happen daily, but this is my view of the Colgate European Women's Open at Sunningdale in 1978 which gave me my first ever opportunity of seeing the top lady professionals of the world competing over seventy-two holes with card and pencil.

What did I think? Well, I was surprised to see such golfing skill, and, except for a handful of them, with limited power too.

Jo-Anne Carner, a big woman of Scandinavian ancestry, hits the ball like a man using a controlled full three-quarter length backswing and with perfect body balance. Another powerful player is gay Nancy Lopez whose Spanish ancestry and skin colouring, powerful play and success remind me of Sevvy Ballesteros. She gives the ball a fantastic whack but with a curious pick-up of the club head from address which I suspect is probably a temporary ploy to correct some weakness. Anyway, she certainly knows her game, and even at her young age (early twenties) the control she shows in her short game must be unique. Her reading of the greens, and of the effects on the flight of the ball when playing from various lies, is unbelievable, quite apart from her instinctive knowledge of how to win.

As the tournament progressed and there was a chance to see them all play it was clear that Nancy Lopez was the one to beat, and I sense this will be the situation for years to come if this attractive girl continues to play, free from injury, and does not make motherhood her main career. One example of her class still comes to the fore as I attempt to recall highlights of the event. It was her opening hole in the final round when leading by three strokes. A long drive down the left side of the fairway finished in a little strip of semi-rough which left her no chance of carrying the two big heather-covered mounds in echelon across the fairway some 80–100 yards from the green on the 480-yard par 5 hole. Those banks are great hazards, the like of which one rarely sees today.

In attempting to play short she again dragged the ball to the left, leaving herself an almost impossible third shot to get at the flag, positioned at the back left of the green and only four or five yards from two deep sand bunkers and the back of the green. But she just had a go

at the stick, 100–1 against getting dead. The ball, only slightly pulled, slid down the bank behind the green to finish on a swampy grass cart track. A free pick and drop (casual water) left a nasty little pitch. A fluffable sort of lie, after the drop, caused her to over-hit the ball a little and it scampered five yards past the hole – this for a par! In it went!

As in any group of people, the proettes come in all sizes and shapes but, no matter what jealousies exist when those who win most live best, once the show is on they behave like actresses. They dress well, hair well styled, and their course manners exemplify the spirit of golf – quite an example to their male counterparts.

The scores at Sunningdale were good. Although the tees and putting surfaces were superb, the fairways had still not full recovered after the drought of 1976, and so the lie of the ball was often poor, limiting the range of shots possible. Because of rain the course played long, which meant that for quite a lot of the players holes like the 409-yard uphill 16th were out of reach in two shots, while the 393-yard uphill 18th needed a wooden club for the second shot.

Of course the stronger players, like Jo-Anne Carner, were able to make good use of their driving power and she was, in fact, the only player to take an iron club off the tee at the 15th (210 yards) and reach the putting surface. She also arrived on some of the difficult longer par 4s with an iron club.

In all categories of golf, particularly when the course is holding the ball, length does help a lot. Consequently the average length strikers – and they make up the majority in any category of players – can only win occasionally, and usually only then by excelling at their short game. This Colgate Women's Open was no exception. Apart from one or two big hitters, power play was not a major feature of the game. But the putting and chipping around and on the greens was superb – accurate, skilful and a real joy to watch.

Many women golfers have to adopt a modified form of the normal swing and to hit side-saddle at impact, so that the arms do not sweep tight across the bosom with the strike and follow-through. This action sequence shows Nancy Lopez taking 'avoiding action' very successfully.

Anyone who has followed her amazing career,

achieving so much while still so young, must wonder how long it can go on. Can she continue to reel off par figures under such pressure? Does she rely too much on her putting? From long years in the game I am suspicious of anyone using such a closed club face action being able to stay at the top. The spine is just not built to withstand such an action, on such a scale; it is all too violent. With a record such as Nancy has produced in her first few years, any critic must tread carefully, but I fear the consequences of these closed-faced swings – especially when they are so upright.

2. How the club face can become so closed without the left wrist hingeing back is already a puzzle. The upper arms, however, are well clear of the body as the club head is pushed away going up.

3. Hands very high, club head pointing well right of the target. I have always seen the advantages of this position if the left wrist is under the shaft, but this position frightens me!

1. All very correct and comfortable at address.

4. Things already looking more normal – so why the contortions in the second and third photographs?

6. Here is the side-saddle impact, hips facing the target even before impact. Club face square, shaft and left arm in line, the arms well clear of the chest. But just look at the twist of the spine! This is the part of the action that can prove so very tough on the back. (I recommend lots of swings 'left-handed' as a 'contra'.)

5. Hands pulling down and through but now well clear of the right hip. Left arm bending a little – rather like Ballesteros.

7. The club face has been held square by the tremendous body effort but now it can all go through. The hands are free to roll, the ball long since gone.

The Invisible Ball

8. And on to a free finish. But still the body has not been pulled upright. If the right shoulder had rolled over a bit and come up it would have eased the strain on the back. Ballesteros's right shoulder rides through much higher – a point in favour of his action.

This is a story of a periodical visitor to the No. 1 course at Sotogrande in Spain who sets out with a full set of clubs and a caddie, and who plays a full round, but who never actually hits a golf ball! He will stick a peg into the first tee, address it (no ball), swing, and then walk to where he has decided his ball has gone. He will then 'play' his next shot from this spot, and so on.

Nor does he give himself the benefit of a perfect round. Occasionally he will reach down into a water hazard, lift out his invisible ball, drop it over his shoulder, and then play another shot. Or, on the green, he will miss a two-foot putt, then shake his putter with aggravation or annoyance.

I became aware of this astonishing character and his unique approach to the game during my time as No. 2 course golf director at Sotogrande. Unfortunately we never got together for a match. It would have been very interesting – especially if he had allowed me to play the same way. I never actually saw him play; this is hearsay.

I am not sure that the present trend towards big money prizes in Pro-Am tournaments is in the best interest of golf. When there are four players in the same team keeping their own scores it cannot be right. Everyone on the professional side seeks to have supporting amateur players with handicaps always just a 'little bit different' from the way they actually play. A man who is 18 and can play for 6 is the ideal Pro-Am partner and now with full-handicap strokes allowance a dozen under par in one round is not at all uncommon.

When a golfer tries to get his right shoulder well under and through he often hits the ground behind the ball and panics. Then he lets his right shoulder ride high and usually gets outside the ball on the way down! But the need to let the right shoulder ride high can be avoided if the player comes up on his toes at impact. This rise is seen quite often in the swings of the top players and is a perfectly good technique.

You can play golf, good golf even, with an unorthodox grip. If you have one, stay with it as long as it works for you. There is no guarantee that you will fare better by changing to a perfect classical grip; you may fare worse.

Few golfers ever practise without seeing the result of their shots by using the eyes and voice of a friend to tell them what has happened to the ball, yet this is a splendid exercise for educating the hands and fingers and developing a real feel for the ball on the club face. Try it sometime, with a 60 yard shot to a post or other convenient marker. Try and hit the ball the desired distance, and with the chosen flight path, without using the eye to judge the shot. Working by feel alone is great fun, quite difficult – and very good training.

Since the advent of moulded rubber grips and the constant steel shaft thickness, players have virtually ceased to experiment with grip thicknesses. Yet in the days of the wrap-round leather grips we would spend quite some time getting the grip of a club just right. Not one player in a thousand has the ideal grip for his hands. A little more attention here might solve a number of players' problems as all hands are different in size for a start.

A bent left elbow going up may suit more golfers than a straight left arm, but, of course, the bent left arm is out of fashion. Try to use it; it could help to get rid of tension in the backswing and also ease some strain on the grip with the fingers.

Percy and Peter

Percy Alliss and his son Peter both played Ryder Cup golf and both were successful tournament players, but if they had one weakness in common it could have been on the greens.

Percy was such a great player in his time, he could have won everything. In fact, at one period in his life I thought he was the greatest and most consistent hitter of a golf ball I had ever seen. He could play for a month, rarely missing a fairway, and never failing to hit a green. He'd find the green with a wood, an iron, anything you like, but there were other players who seemed to get the ball in the hole in fewer strokes. At times, however, he was unbeatable. At Wannsee Golf Club in Berlin, Germany, before the war, three pro teams from Britain, America and the Continent went to play a 72-hole medal event on this beautiful pine forest course where he was pro, and he won by the length of a street! The group picture was taken at Wannsee in 1929. Percy Alliss is on the extreme left and I am second from right. Percy held the club beautifully, as you can see in this iron shot. He's played it cleanly, hardly taking a divot, to 'throw' the ball at the flag with beautiful control.

Peter was cast in a much bigger mould, and had a neat simple action with which he hit the ball straight and a long way. He was an outstanding stylist and one always wondered why he too didn't win everything in his time, but finally he realized that it wasn't worth suffering on the putting greens, where he had very mixed success. Quite rightly he turned to other facets of the golf game where he is still a star – a worthy T.V. commentator and successor to Henry Longhurst, an author and golf course architect.

Percy Alliss

Peter Alliss

Bringing It Square

Gary Player, the powerful 5ft 9in South African golf wizard, comes into the ball. This is the point of the swing which interests everyone. How does any top golfer bring the club face square to the ball from waist high?

The club face is directly to the front in the first picture. How then does he deliver the blow square? The fact is that the hands and the wrists have to be trusted to do this on their own. There is just no other way. Can anyone doubt this? No body action can be expected to do this, for the hands have moved forward very little. In the second picture they must have almost 'stopped' for the club head to catch up to square. Forget any notion of your body action achieving this. It can't!

Finding the ball, the back centre of it with the centre of the club face, is all you are setting out to do. Your swing, if it does not make this easy, must be wrong; try another one.

Is it more enjoyable to pull a caddie cart full of clubs than to carry fewer clubs in a Sunday bag? This is a very controversial point, but a golfer walks fewer yards carrying his own clubs and I believe the bending down, lifting up of the bag is a perfect contra exercise to the one-way violent twist of the spine.

It is better to fall back at impact rather than lean into the shot (unless you are driving the ball down) and hit up and over, like a forehand drive at table tennis.

Henry Longhurst once observed that Bobby Locke's putts had a better lick off the club face than those of most of his contemporaries, even with the softer ball of his day. I putt well and enjoy putting even more today because I love the hard click of the modern ball off the club face. That sharp knock, almost like an auctioneer's hammer, is one of the thrills of the game. I often wonder how we putted as well as we did with a ball that left the club with the sound and feel of sponge rubber!

It is excellent contra exercise to dangle on a bar regularly during the day and to sleep without a pillow occasionally. The condition of the spine is all-important : it needs a good stretch now and then.

Working at Control

Those who watched Cotton in the thirties were privileged to see a simplicity of style and a contained power and accuracy of striking, with wood and long-iron especially, that has never been surpassed
PAT WARD-THOMAS

Here I am chipping from the back of the first green at Purley Downs, that famous old downland course near Croydon in Surrey. On the green, holding his putter, is Charlie Johns who was the club's professional for many years. Charlie played his golf by instinct; he loved the game and could chip and putt well as though it was the easiest part of it. He *had* to chip and putt well, because he was on the fragile side and not long enough off the tee for big golf courses.

The picture shows me playing with my right index finger and thumb actually on the metal of the club shaft, in order to get the maximum sensitivity for this delicate shot. Obviously I've just pinched the ball. It must have been a slightly hanging lie, so I couldn't do better than to stab the ball. The practical lesson is that if you are a bit clumsy around the green, don't hesitate to get down the shaft.

In this other photograph I am not demonstrating an underhand throw to the wicket keeper but trying to explain to a pupil how the

right arm has to control even the most delicate shots. Throwing the ball will help him to judge distance, and improve accuracy, by teaching the hand nearest the head to feel the distance, particularly when pacing out the distance is of no value. Once a golfer learns to throw the ball, the next thing is to get him to try to do the same thing with a club in his hand and then add that to his left hand and see if he can get an idea of how the right hand can help in finding the ball and in guiding the club. The push action has a limited value in teaching beginners feel, for it can only succeed when a wide take-away is possible, that is when the lie of the ball is perfect.

Indoors in Dublin

Back in 1928 I was asked to teach and give golf demonstrations in a store in Dublin. I think that in general I had a successful week teaching, but what did I know of golf at the age of twenty-one? Really not very much more than my own game. Still, I always put the accent on a good grip and the correct hand action and those are always good points to pass on.

When I look at this picture, it is hard to realize that quarter of an hour later I was carried to the hospital room in this store. A big, strong Irishman, thoughtless beyond belief, drove off the mat whilst I was picking up the balls at the far end of the net. He hadn't noticed me there and hit a full drive which hit me, luckily I suppose, on the back of my calf and felled me. I didn't know where to put myself with agony and was carried up to the store's medical centre, laid out and given a sedative of some sort while the bruise was attended to. You would hardly expect to come so close to a knockout teaching in a net!

Not long after this the P.G.A. barred golf pros from teaching in stores. It was considered that the big stores should be treated as 'enemies' of the club pro, as they sold golf equipment. This policy has often been given as an example of the 'closed shop', but if defending your own piece of bread is right then the policy has to be accepted.

I Can't Make This Work For Me

Study this picture sequence of one of America's top professionals, Miller Barber, and if you looked only at the last one you would no doubt feel that here is a fellow with a perfect impact position, hitting an ordinary shot straight down the middle of a fairway. But if you look at the contortions he's been through, seen in the first three pictures, you might well wonder why he bothers to do a backswing at all! You might think he'd do better to start at the top and come straight down. In the second picture, where he's got his right elbow rising as the club goes back, with both wrists completely blocking the opening of the face, one wonders how he can possibly be a world class golfer. Yet he is.

The explanation for this complicated action is that early in life Barber had an accident which makes a normal backswing physically impossible. So he settled for this rather extraordinary lift-up of the club, with the face as shut as is possible,

---

Never be ashamed to take a club with which you *know* you can reach the flag even if you fail to make a 100 per cent contact. Settle for the fact that you rarely hit a perfect shot. Even the master swinger Sam Snead reckons on hitting only six perfect shots in a round, even when he's breaking course records. Ben Hogan and I also agreed that half a dozen shots per round *quite* as we envisaged at address was the best we could hope for.

James Braid always claimed that the straightfaced cleek was no good, it should have 10 degrees of loft on the club face to be useful. He could play this longer shafted club, a No. 1 iron of today, like a driver. Many top pros use these cleek-shaped No. 1s, nothing new under the sun, for their tee shots. The loft aiding the 'gripping' of the ball on the face for control

Increased back-spin is imparted by striking the ball smartly and for that reason a light-headed club can be very useful. Some of the wizards around the green keep a favourite lightweight club, not usually part of the set, for the occasional shot where maximum back-spin is required.

The explosion shot from sand was the soundest way to recover from a bunker situation before the arrival of the broad-soled niblick which allowed the ball to be 'splashed' out. In the old days the ball was simply shocked out of a bad sand lie as the club head was buried into the sand behind it. This is still done today but many players prefer the splash shot with the club head skidding underneath the ball, but if the sand is firm forget the sand iron, leave it in the bag. An open faced 9 iron might be best.

A Real Look at the Ball!

Dale Hayes of South Africa, a tall golfer with a casual three-quarter swing and a flashing wrist action, sends the ball a long way and makes it all look so easy, yet his method (a very good one I feel) gets very little appreciation. It has to look difficult, I often think, to please some golf teachers.

Dale is really looking at the ball here, and the bending of the left arm is part of this long-look-at-the-ball action; it guarantees the club face being held square for a long time through the ball. He has used his knees for a timely drop of the arc to bring the club face to the back of the ball. All tall golfers have used a deliberate narrowing of the down swing arc to get a clean attack on the ball or just behind it. Players should remember to aim half an inch behind the ball for all short shots. The ball will then make contact with the club face higher up the blade.

after which he brings it square to the ball with a marvellous instinctive use of the right hand. Then, with his head down, he hits past the chin in the most classical way. It makes every student wonder why he or she is striving to achieve a 'perfect' backswing after all. So, if you've tried everything and failed and you still can't play as you want, here's something you could try. But keep it as a last resort – I simply *cannot* make it work!

Top pro Bernard Gallagher became a convert to the Cotton philosophy after a three-year spell playing below his best form. He said 'I was of the same mind as many others who had become successful tournament players, in that I tried to retain the same tricks and techniques that had stood me in good stead in the past. Now I firmly believe that a swing that no longer works should be dropped and that it pays to re-think – to use the body you have today and to adjust your play to the capabilities of your ageing chassis.'

Arnold Palmer's swing was known as being fast, too violent, and not very attractive. But as he held the club in a vice-like grip he was not wristy: he played with a 'wooden' action through the ball – an action which no one has succeeded in copying.

Inside Out!

Complete scores on the tournament play of individuals, for the three days, including two rounds in the finals, follow. Asterisks designate amateurs:

	1	2	3	4	Total
Tommy Armour, Washington, D. C.	74	66	74	75	289
John Golden, New Jersey	74	69	77	73	293
T. H. Cotton, London, England	74	75	69	78	296
Horton Smith, Joplin, Mo.	70	77	76	74	297
Eddie Loos, Pasadena	70	75	77	75	297
Ed Gayer, Chicago	70	77	79	74	300
Willard Huchinson, Pasadena	78	74	74	74	300
Mortie Dutra, Tacoma	75	78	72	75	300
Al Espinosa, Chicago	76	73	76	75	300
Craig Wood, Newark, N. J.	76	75	76	74	301
Frank Walsh, Appleton, Wis.	76	75	72	78	301
Willie Goggin, San Francisco	73	75	76	78	302
Phil Hesler, Tulsa, Okla.	77	74	78	74	303
Ed Dudley, Los Angeles	74	78	76	75	303
Frank Minch, Sacramento	76	73	76	79	304
*John W. Dawson, Chicago	77	73	78	76	304
Babe McHugh, San Francisco	76	76	77	76	305
Abe Espinosa, Chicago	73	78	77	77	305
Billie Burke, New York	78	76	77	74	305
Ben Richter, St. Louis	79	78	75	73	305
Bob Shave, Cleveland	78	74	78	76	306
Henry Puget, Del Monte	77	76	73	80	306
John Rodger, Denver	75	76	75	81	307

When I went to America for the first time in November 1928, I noticed that in general the top players were all hitting the ball from inside to out with a draw. The large ball in use there had to be hit this way and the dedicated American professionals, many of them much bigger fellows than myself, hit the ball quite a lot further and only used the balls which just went through a 1·68-inch gauge which every pro carried in his bag, i.e., the minimum legal size.

At that time I was, in fact, hitting the ball with a slice which I had developed through practising in our narrow family garage in London. That was the only place I had to play in as I could not get on a golf course as often as I liked. I practised for hours every night, hitting balls from a mat into a net, but the garage, being narrow, made my swing very upright. Whilst in America I realized I had to alter my angle of backswing. Although I finished third in my first U.S. tournament, the Sacramento Open, and played quite well with my hickory shafts against the rest of the field using the new steel ones, I lost really through lack of experience and because I could not handle the larger ball with my slice-prone upright swing in rough weather.

So I set out to learn how to hit the ball from the inside, and this was a movement that I practised all the time, trying to get my hands down somewhere near my right leg with my right shoulder under and the attack well inside the line, practising the pull down endlessly without a ball, just to make sure I kept on the inside. Then if I had the club face a little more turned in, or even square, I had no difficulty getting the ball to fly with a draw. Of course, I was falling between two stools for quite a while, but by the time I started home from Florida in early April 1929 I really had quite a nice draw going which I think surprised people, as I was hitting a much longer ball off the tee.

It is rather curious that the photograph of myself taken in 1929 or 1930 makes a perfect pair with the more recent one of Gary Player demonstrating the same point: how to keep the club on the inside coming down. Of course he knows, as I knew, that you cannot play golf if you get into this exaggerated camera pose, but it is the idea to have in your mind when you are starting from the top. Get the right elbow and forearm going forward, leading, so that the club head is held back and then you can hit the ball from inside to out.

Gary Player

Find the Ball

Most people are still taught that the ideal way to play golf is to acquire a swing and to use that swing, and that once you have it, it is there forever. This is, of course, very wrong.

The thing that really counts is to find the ball, accurately and consistently, and that means teaching golfers to handle a golf club as if it were an extension of the arms. It need not be one specific series of movements; it can be any movement which will deliver the head of the golf club to the back of the ball squarely, or at the chosen angle at that moment.

Finding the ball simply means bringing the club head square to the ball, at the height at which the ball is lying. You do not always need to take a divot, nor do you need to swing always to one height. Your aim is to guide the club face to the back of the ball. Just look how Peter Thomson has used his left elbow to raise his hit just enough to get a solid impact. This is a perfect illustration of what is meant by finding the ball. Ballesteros can be observed with his left arm bending at this point in the swing too.

The Price to Pay

What twenty-five years at the top has done for Arnold Palmer! He has become a legend in his life-time. He has played dashing golf, which has made him the most popular golfer of all time with the public. He has made a fortune with his triumphs all over the world. He is now over fifty years old and these photographs show that time has taken its toll; the mileage is showing. Will he be able to carry on at the same pace or will he slow up? From fifty to fifty-five is a crucial age for men. Arnie apparently intends to carry on in medal play golf. 'What else can I do that I enjoy as much as competitive golf?' he says, but will he go on taking the punishment? Time will tell.

Arnold has all manner of business interests and his extraordinary physical prowess and good health have enabled him to get the maximum out of his life. He still strikes the ball well but with the usual middle-age change of sight, putting has become a problem, a torture even!

He is the latest Honorary Member of the Royal and Ancient Golf Club of St Andrews – one of the game's greatest honours.

More Sam Snead

This action, plus the power and flexibility he has, makes Sam Snead everybody's ideal golfer.

Points to study: left knee inwards, left heel raised; right hip pulled back and right leg straight; left shoulder down, left arm extended (but *not forced stiff*); back of the left arm in line with the back of the hand; club face almost fully open; right elbow well clear of the body and pointing down; club shaft horizontal.

I like to see the left elbow just pointing forwards a little, as seen here, not down to the ground – this is worth a try, particularly for those who hit too many off the toe of the club! But always remember, this is not the action a champion guarantees to use every time he plays, he has to vary his method slightly, to get everything that moves in harmony.

Only for a Few – Square to Square

Arnold Palmer, one of the game's great individualists, used this top of the swing hand action, club face facing the sky, regularly and very successfully, but it was not generally seen as being an action suited to only an exceptionally powerful golfer. In fact, it's a technique used with success by only a few. Yet it was 'sold' by the golf profession, through the teachers of the game, in articles and golf books everywhere for many years. I always saw great danger in this action. It is out of fashion now, but even today it is being sold by some teachers, but few players can make it work. It is only for a giant trying to guide his ball, not the ordinary golfer seeking more length, for it goes with a push stroke not a whip.

David Thomas, that amiable giant of British pro golf for some years, used it successfully, but eventually 'knocked his back up' and that brought his career to a halt. Note how his left wrist has twisted to close the club face.

Arnold Palmer

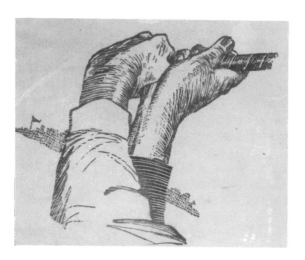

A very flexible shaft encourages a golfer to wait for the impact, not to lash the ball. But I have noticed there is but one speed for the swing. The stroke cannot be forced with a whippy shaft. I can use a super whippy shaft if I stick to one lazy tempo, but when I try to force the ball a bit I get problems and often mis-hit. The only value of the whippy shaft is to teach rhythm. Professionals favour a stiff shaft because it means that they *can* force a shot without any danger of mis-timing.

David Thomas

Our Best Course

Very few of my memories have the clubhouse and 18th green at Muirfield looking as peaceful and deserted as this, for on tournament days it is alive with tents, milling crowds and an atmosphere of excitement.

It is one of the great golf courses of the world. The bunker with the grass island on the right side of the final hole has always been a terror. I have been in it, and in fact it is possible to get the ball lodged in a position from which you simply cannot get a shot to the flag – or even to the green. My most memorable visit to that bunker was in the 1948 Open when I took two to get out of it on the 72nd hole of The Open. But I managed to get down in one putt for a five. Muirfield is in fact my favourite course – always in perfect condition and cruelly fair! Jack Nicklaus must also have it high up on his own list of great courses for he named his vast golfing complex in Ohio, Muirfield.

Here I am putting at the third hole at Muirfield, a natural grandstand.

It Works!

If you want your bunker shot to pop out of the sand and land steeply with maximum back-spin, screw the club face under the ball with the right hand at the moment the blade makes contact with the sand. This may sound a complicated shot but it can in fact be learned very easily and is a valuable asset to any player.

A No. 2 wood with a lofted face is easier to use from the tee than a driver. Not because the club itself is very different but because the ball, even when not struck perfectly in the centre of the face, will become airborne more easily. The impact shock on the hands is reduced because the loft allows the ball to slide up the club face. For this same reason it is easier to play lofted irons, up to the No. 4, than the lower numbered irons.

It has always struck me that sets of wooden clubs should have two drivers; one with a stiffer and stronger shaft than the other, but they can both have the same loft. On warm days, when all is going well, the stronger shaft would probably work better, just as a higher compression ball (100) is best when it is warm.

I have always been interested in how golfers would play if they went on using the grip all children instinctively adopt, left hand below the right, when they first handle a club and hit a ball. Later they are shown how to play 'correctly'! But what is correct? I have never known of anyone being *taught* this grip, but if you wanted an 'odd grip' this is what you would do: place the left hand *below* the right, but it can be effective! It is becoming fashionable for putting.

There was a professional, a coloured South African boy, named Sewsunker Sewgolum, who played with this grip and he won the Dutch Open from a strong field using it. But whenever I have tried it I have found that the club has to slip a lot in the hands to be able to make contact.

The man in the photograph, low handicap golfer Rufus Evans, has got the club *very* shut at the top, and the hands have slipped on the grip during the upswing. But it takes all sorts to make a world, and what might look the hard way to most people invariably proves to be the natural way for somebody.

Half the Game

I hadn't been long in golf before I realized that putting is more or less half the game. It can be more than half if you're not a good putter, in terms of the proportion of putts versus other strokes taken per round, it can be less if you're a superb putter, but it has to be done, you cannot avoid putting. You have to get the ball into the hole and as you can't pitch it straight in, you have to roll it along the ground. The theory and practice of putting has occupied a lot of my time and a lot of my thought over the years.

The earliest picture I have of myself putting was taken on the practice green at Langley Park Golf Club, Beckenham, Kent, where I was pro, aged nineteen. I used for a time a wooden putter with a slightly hollow face, and did quite well with it, but it was later ruled illegal for a golf club to have a hollow or curved face. The club had a hickory shaft and I am using a reverse overlapping grip. This was the way I thought I ought to train – to try and hit the ball like a machine. I did everything to become a machine. I marked the position of my fingers on the shaft so

that I had the same grip every day; I marked the positions of my feet on a piece of material so my stance never varied; I always had the ball in the same address spot, so that I could get exactly the same address position for each putt. All went well for a while, and then suddenly it didn't work! Putting, I found, was simply not that mechanical, not a science but an art.

But I was determined to master putting, so from a method with a wristy action, which seemed very natural, I changed to as stiff-armed an action as I could. Everything moved in one block. I used the reverse overlap again, placed the ball opposite the left toe so as to have a fixed position, blocked my wrists, and then moved the whole top of the body through in one piece with the elbows held locked and spread out. This worked reasonably well for short putts, but I had trouble trying to keep my hands out of it with long approach putts as I had lost a lot of feel. But I persevered with this method and had some successes, especially with the old aluminium putter which helped me win the 1934 Open. It is

The 1934 Open

now in the United States Golf Association Museum! (The cameraman wanted to get a new angle of ball rolling into the hole, and this was the position he chose.)

As the years went by I enjoyed more than ever experimenting and tried all sorts of odd putters and methods. I found I could save a lot of strokes by using my favourite blade putter as a 'Texas wedge' from off-green positions when I could get the ball rolling rather than pitching it. And then there was the stand upright putter style I used for a while, holding the club against my stomach and just moving my right hand to and fro. It worked, and then it didn't work, so that was one I didn't stick to for very long. But it was fun and it gave me hope and that is what we all are looking for. Then a friend, a former 'twitcher' himself, showed me an anti-twitch grip which I also tried, out of interest. I never actually developed a twitch, but I think if I had gone on playing tournament golf longer I would have caught the disease in the end, as many other people have done.

The first twitcher I ever saw was Harry Vardon, who, towards the end of his life, had to

be given every putt of three feet or under as he simply couldn't hit the hole. The ball used to fly off to the right at the most impossible angles and at an unpredictable distance too, so quite rightly Harry just picked up the ball for a 'gimmee' – and no questions asked!

James Braid followed suit soon after, and some twitch he had! He began hitting too many putts which didn't touch the hole from three feet and less, so he just walked to the ball. majestically picked it up and then insisted, almost insultingly, that you hole out. He used to say that picking up the ball was only for old gentlemen who didn't need to test themselves, and now I regret that I find myself doing it, because it is such a bother and strain to concentrate hard on knocking in those two- and three-footers.

However, the value of good putting hasn't really changed. You still have to hit the ball into the hole and the old dictums – 'A man who can putt is a match for anyone', 'Matches are won on the greens' and 'Scores are made on the greens' – are all as true today as ever, and always will be providing we stick to a $4\frac{1}{2}$ in. hole.

'Stiff-armed' putting

Using my favourite blade putter
as a 'Texas wedge'

The 'stand upright' putter style

An anti-twitch grip

This Putting Game

Jack Nicklaus practising using an action based on a push of the ball with the weight of his right arm – a piston-like stroke.

Dr J. A. Flaherty using a putt 'off the right toe' stance. A very open stance method which keeps the body very still and, for some, makes lining up the putt easier.

Neil Coles putts with a very shut-to-open action – a big hinge.

A BETTER WAY TO PUTT?

THE PUTTING STYLE OF THE FUTURE?

(Note Grip)

"**PUTTING –**

A NEW APPROACH"

Revised Edition

$1.00

Postpaid

PUTTING

Box 955

Okla. City 1, Okla.

In this method, supposed to be anti-twitch, the right hand works sideways. I have tried it but with limited success, although I have seen others use it effectively.

Sam Snead adopted this style as an anti-twitch method, before long it was ruled illegal – I never knew why – and now he putts side-saddle. His hold of the club is interesting.

Archie Compston was a fine putter who pushed his left elbow towards the hole and hinged his wrists, keeping the weight on his left foot.

Gary Player has just holed a good one and started a fashion of the clenched fist method of celebrating – much copied by the youth of today!

Ben Crenshaw, considered one of the soundest putters in America. This 'take away with the left hand' finish helps to keep the line for long putts and works in fact for all sorts of shots to the flag. This is of course the end of a hit with the *right* hand, which seems paradoxical to some.

An experienced old golfer, who stands with shoulders facing the hole and putts the ball almost at right angles to the way he faces.

Tall Tom Weiskopf – a reverse overlap grip using a putter with a very upright stance.

Sam Torrance, one of the better young pros, uses the reverse hands grip on his putter.

Bobby Locke and His Hook

Bobby Locke, some thirty years ago, had perhaps the most renowned hook in first class golf. In this photograph he is aiming right off at the three people seen alongside the wood, fully expecting the ball to finish close to the cross on the left. I do not remember ever seeing him fail to bring it round despite his enormous 'aim off'. I played many times with him and became quite familiar with this extraordinary position at the top of the swing. He had a shallow-faced club and yet he rarely skied the ball. He just hit the ball cleanly off the top with his extraordinary swinging hook and brought it round to the target as if by radar. I do not suppose there are many professional golfers in the world today who could pull off a similar shot for a bet with any guarantee of getting anywhere near the target.

From the time he was very young and slim Locke must have had this natural hook from a top-of-the-swing position with the club head practically over the ball. As you can see, he has the club head well round with the club face open, and yet he manages to give the ball the distance and the flight path he wants. But he could not produce a controlled cut shot. This action of his is hitting inside to out *par excellence*. If you stood across a ball like that, aiming far to the right, you would not, generally speaking, be able to get your face hooded enough to bring the ball back. Yet Locke did this quite naturally, from an open face too! Remarkable, for the ball although flying with a big hook did not run very much, it seemed to 'feather' down.

Whenever I am talking to someone troubled by a slice I stress that golf is a two-handed game and the hands must work together. If for any reason they do not, then the right hand, which should be able to hood the face instinctively and bring the ball back, is blocked by the left hand. To such players I always say, 'If you were playing tennis and I bounced you a tennis ball you would never slice it into the garden on the right, would you? You would just roll your right arm over to any degree needed, and bring the ball back to the left side of the court or hit it wherever you chose.' But give that person two hands on a golf club and his right hand is immediately blocked by the left, and so he still goes on slicing.

The secret of getting rid of your slice is to make your left hand square the club face on its own. Then you learn how to add the right hand so that it does not stop the left doing the necessary movement to bring the club face square. It is important to get this left-hand action fixed in your mind. As Bob Goalby, who was a top class American tournament player in his time, explains, 'It is just like thumbing a lift with the left hand. The left hand does not follow on through straight, it bends at the elbow and the thumb flicks to the left at the finish.' Not a bad picture to have in mind.

I have always thought it would be nice to offer golfers a round at St Andrews using a copy set of hickory-shafted clubs, similar to those used by the golfing heroes of yesteryear, and a ball of similar size and compression to those of the period. For that, they would get a certificate when they completed the round. Golfers just do not realize what fun the game was in those days, and how difficult.

Harry Vardon's big fleshy hands looked comfortable on the grip, for he overlapped, of course, the little finger of the right hand on the index finger of the left hand. I do believe, however, that J. H. Taylor was the first player to use this grip successfully, even though it was not named after him. Vardon, who was the more elegant player, has been given credit for inventing this grip and 'J. H.' was always a little bit hurt about the credit going to his friend and rival.

When You Must Aim to Miss the Ball

In golf today, where most courses are built on open farm or park land, the architect relies heavily on strategically placed sand hazards to make his layout a real test. Some courses have dozens of bunkers, others seem to be adequate tests with far fewer, but rarely is a round played without a player getting his ball into the sand at some time. The low-scoring tournament players go for the pin no matter where on the green it is located because they are not frightened of being obliged to play a recovery shot from the sand. Thickish rough is often much more difficult on a bunker bottom than sand. The nearer the flag is to a bunker, the easier the shot becomes. The more distant the flag, the more difficult is the shot when the ball is lying in sand.

The first point to remember in trying to become proficient as a bunker player is that these are precision strokes, they are not 'hit and hope' efforts, which is why many beginners and high handicap players are so scared of finding their ball in sand. They are not sure of striking into the sand correctly.

The skid sole on the modern sand wedge has simplified sand recovery play and once a player has got used to the effect of the sole he can play shot after shot to the hold side, almost as easily as if he were chipping from short grass. Practice facilities from sand are non-existent at most clubs, but if practice is carried out from a bunker in a quiet corner of the course, I doubt if there would be too many complaints, as long as the sand is raked after, or how can a player learn?

I recently played out of a bunker for a slow-motion camera shot and I found the sand in this particular bunker to be pale and dry, rather coarse in texture but clean, with no large stones or pebbles in it (I was observing and taking in information even before I took my stance). This kind of sand is not the easiest to play from, but experienced golfers will have met it before. More sand will collect between club face and ball and therefore more power is needed for this shot than for one on heavy wet sand.

As I take up my stance I screw my feet as deeply and as firmly as possible into the sand, to find out how much depth there is, for I am not permitted to touch the sand with my club or do practice swings in an adjoining bunker. Apart from using my eyes, this is my only legal way of obtaining information. Then I place my feet so that the ball lies in the position from which I calculate I can best play the shot I have already visualized. Far too many golfers just slap aimlessly at the ball, they know they are not accurate enough to aim the necessary one inch, two inches, or even more, behind the ball, so they just hit and hope. I teach my pupils sand recovery shots by making marks behind balls placed in a bunker and making them look at the mark, not at the ball.

Golfers can become so used to aiming at the ball that even when concentrating on a spot well behind it, they let their eyes drift to the ball itself at the last second and so hit it just as they would hit a pitch shot from the turf. They hit the ground after touching the ball, not before it, which achieves nothing except a skinned shot which sends the ball miles over the green if play is from a green-side bunker.

In soft sand, top players have the ball well on the left toe to help them to strike the sand before the ball, but in order to get the sole of the club to splash into the sand when the ball lies so far forward, a sort of downward knee slide, with both knees, is really essential. It is also a safe way of judging the amount of 'dig down' into the sand, because the strong thigh muscles are able to control the depth of the 'curtsey' quite easily.

The Walker Cup Match 1938

Writing has been an interesting and enjoyable sideline to my playing career and over the years I have written a number of articles on the amateur game .Invitations to write seem to abound once you become a 'name'. I attended many events, and was one of the few professionals who took any interest in amateur golf. I saw the Walker Cup matches a number of times and when I was Open Champion I even went to help train the Walker Cup Team because I thought if the home players could beat me we had a chance against America.

I went to St Andrews at my own expense in 1938 and played with members of the Great Britain and Ireland team in turn. John Beck was the Captain and his big worry was that I would upset his star, Jimmy Bruen, then eighteen years old, a boy from Cork who hit the ball a country mile. I told John Beck, 'I don't want to play with Bruen if you think I'm going to upset his game.' But Jimmy insisted he wanted to play with me, he wanted to compare himself with me to see how good he was. I was twice Open Champion and current holder at the time. Finally John Beck said, 'Well, you can have a game with him as long as you don't tell him anything that will put him off.' I said, 'This boy is about to have the game of his life in the Walker Cup match. He doesn't need to be told how to play.'

When we went out on the course we had half of St Andrews there. I played as well as I could play at the time and went round in 69. Jimmy also returned a 69 and I was terribly impressed with his play. Britain won the Walker Cup for the first time that year and I like to think my training helped.

Home Captain John Beck (left) and Francis Quimet, United States, hold the Walker Cup

You can show the palm of the right hand as viewed from the tee box at the very top of the backswing if it helps a full wrist cock. If the club is held in the fingers then the hand can be opened with no harmful effects. But the shaft must not be loosened and regripped.

Some players allow the club shaft to slip in the 'V' between the right forefinger and thumb at the top of the swing if the right wrist cannot cock in the normal way. Dai Rees is one top player who has always done this – and with a double-handed grip too.

Remember that you do not knock the ball off the line with your right hand. If the right hand is in charge then, provided the left hand gets out of the way so that the right can guide the club face properly, you should be able to hit the ball with complete confidence.

Driving is the easiest part of the golf game. The distance you achieve might be useful but it is not as important as many players seem to think. It is far more important to get the direction right and to be able to give the ball a desired trajectory.

Sand Play

Billy Casper

What many club golfers do not realize is that for short distance recoveries from sand (and even from loose sandy fairway lies and 'flip up' pitch shots) the right hand must work the club face under the ball as seen in the action shots of Mark James and Billy Casper. James's ball can be seen flying high in the air already, as if it had been thrown up by hand.

In these strokes, there is no doubt that the right hand is in charge. The left wrist has hinged back to help the action. This stroke, whilst looking complicated, can be learned in a few minutes in a bunker (or even in green-side rough). I have taught thousands of golfers how to play it. Gary Player, indisputedly the greatest sand player, says, 'It is *all* right hand'. High handicap golfers have to learn to skid the sole of the club into the sand and then screw the face under the ball, once sufficient depth has been obtained for the blade to skid under it.

I have never seen a better photograph than the one of Mark James to illustrate this essential hand action in the stroke. It is a must for everyone.

Valentin Barrios of Spain is screwing the face open on this pitch shot to get height on his ball and to guarantee the ball will stay on, or right of, the target.

Valentin Barrios

Mark James

Putting It Over

I think that every professional should spend some time teaching golf. It is a great way to learn more about the game and in any case it is a profitable way of filling the day, because no one can hit golf balls eight hours a day every day. I think this is one of the mistakes many of our young players make, they over-practise. They don't learn the game thoroughly and they just can't fill in the hours. They set up too much fatigue and end up doing too much practice with tired muscles. If they get tired they practise aimlessly, going through the motions without really concentrating. I have found over the years that people who stand around a lot, and most golf teachers accept this as part of their profession, get very tired – especially in the legs and back. There really is no need to stand if you can sit; and there is no need to sit when you can lie. I think Winston Churchill used this expression many times!

Here I am just about to start teaching somebody and, for my preliminary chat, I have got myself into a comfortable position so that I can enjoy the lesson without getting absolutely fatigued. For a senior it is fine, but perhaps for a young pro it might look a bit lazy. But standing up is exhausting and you certainly can't teach well at the end of a day when your legs are aching. Of course, I enjoy popping up and down and giving a demonstration, and I really do sympathize with any teacher who can't *show* his pupil. One of the great joys, and one of the great credits to the teacher, is when he can say to the pupil, 'Now this is what you are trying to do. This is how I work my hands. This is how I hit the ball. This is where my left hand finishes when I use it on its own, and this is where my right hand finishes.'

Most people think the only thing that matters in golf is hitting full shots, but I like to take my pupil along from the beginning and teach him that feel and touch are his most important assets, and that he must work to develop them. In the photograph a pupil is learning to do just that. He is holding the club well down the grip and is being shown that this shot is almost a putt, even though he has a No. 6 iron in his hand. He is trying to pitch the ball onto a spot on the green, which should just give it enough flight to clear the intervening longer grass and then skid

forward to the hole. These shots are guesses of course; how hard you hit the ball and what flight you give it can only be gained from experience.

In the other two photographs I am teaching the left hand to *hit* the ball back-handed, not to push it. I am showing a seventeen-year-old 1 handicap player how to start building up his weak hands on the tyre with a gripped shaft, no head. This encourages speed and is easier as a start, when the hands quit on impact too readily. It is quite tiring too!

Below, young Ian Matthews is doing his left-hand drill. 'Hit the tyre back-handed – but do *not* touch my stick with your left hand!' I was telling him.

Tom Watson

Everything about this good-looking, auburn-haired, freckle-faced young player would make him an ideal hero for the *Boy's Own Paper* – one of those long-extinct schoolboy magazines I used to love so much as a boy. He is strongly built, quite tall (I ruined my posture as a youth through playing too much golf without contra exercises) and has that bouncy, elastic walk that goes with powerful legs.

His golf action is just right. It looks right, and it works – as his record proves beyond doubt. No excessive wrist action but just enough to produce maximum club head speed. He uses his feet better than many of his contemporaries – raising the left heel to help his body turn freely. The only really personal part of his swing is the finish: he finishes with both knees bent no matter what shot he has played. Byron Nelson claimed that he also used this bent knee finish because he felt the knee action was like an extra wrist movement.

Tom is one of the most 'complete' of the young players of today; his putting is superb and he has a marvellous future in the game. He is a fellow with college degrees, intelligent in an academic way, so I guess he has already planned his career, for when he cannot win regularly he will stop banging his head against a wall.

Golf on the tour, travelling continuously, is not living, it is existing, even if you can do it in the greatest comfort.

Every golfer who gets round in par will still cry about the two or three putts he missed. That's life!

Too many golfers find short approaches and bunker shots and putts quite boring, the only real joy they get in golf is bashing the ball.

Just check this: most golfers have a club slip in their right hands. Does yours move? Many of my pupils do not want to know about it, they want to learn something else. They do not want to be told that they have to work on the right hand until they can hold the club firmly with it when they strike the ball. I even put a thin right-hand mitt on some of my pupils, just to prove to them that their right hand was sliding when they tried to hit the ball. This different feel helped the gloved left hand to build up a complete non-slip grip with both hands.

Looking at the Ball at Sotogrande

Fate took me for two happy years (1955–7) to Sotogrande in the south of Spain where I first met Mr Joe McMicking, the founder and owner of the magnificent 4,000-acre Sotogrande development. He asked me if I would run the new golf club there and I stayed two years with him at the superb Robert Trent Jones golf course. The course is beautifully manicured and has the most perfect greens, but it is just too testing; that is my only real criticism. In this picture Joe McMicking putts while I hold the flag on the 7th green with the luxurious clubhouse dining room, capacity for 200 people, in the background. This grandiose club has every facility one could wish for, as well as a most wonderful practice ground where you drive into a valley, which is of course always flattering.

In the photo of me driving on the practice area of Sotogrande I have demonstrated my swing where I hit past my chin as usual. I have always been a good looker at the ball, because I have a loose neck and keep well away from the ball at address, so that I can swing the club freely, without my body interfering with my hitting arc. By the way, remember, if you can, never to swing with your lungs full of air; empty your lungs – blow out – before you start the backswing. This is for all shots.

The Bruen Loop

Jimmy Bruen was an Irish boy from Cork, exceptionally strong, though he didn't look it. He was six feet tall, with powerful sloping shoulders. He had the most extraordinary looping swing I have ever seen. The majority of people who saw him swing said, 'How can anyone play golf with the club head right over the ball at the top of the swing?' It looked an almost normal take-away at first, but then went on and on, until suddenly the shaft and the club head went forward over his head. Then he brought the club down on an inside arc and gave the ball a really terrible smash. Some of the shots he hit can never have been bettered, or even equalled, in the history of golf. Some of them took place at St Andrews, so it is possible to compare some of his feats with what goes on today. He regularly won his age group of throwing the cricket ball – his best throw being over ninety yards. I have found that anyone who can throw a ball well can hit it well. This could be a reason why Americans who throw well at baseball find golf easy.

Just before the war Jimmy was playing off + 6 against the Standard Scratch Score so, as you can well imagine, he was quite a golfer. He could play all departments of the game well and when I first saw him he was in the 1938 Walker Cup Team. He played No. 1 in Great Britain's singles and foursomes and, whilst he didn't actually win his singles match against the best player in the U.S. team, Charlie Yates, he only just lost, but he was a great inspiration to the team. I made a pre-match statement, saying I didn't think anybody in the U.S. team could beat this boy.

He wanted me to see him swing and this is the photograph of the first shot I ever saw him hit. He kept his head down a long time, extra long perhaps to impress me because I was Open Champion at the time and playing in practice rounds with the members of the British team to see if I couldn't toughen them up.

Most people who saw this swing of his said he wouldn't last, but I saw immediately that when he got to the top, his right elbow came down to his right hip and his hands flashed the club head through with such speed that the ball was hit with the biggest carry you have ever seen – up to 300 yards. On the present long 15th 530 yards of the championship course at Royal Birkdale, Southport, I saw him pitch the ball onto that green with two woods – and that was on a damp day. The ball pitched right onto the heart of the green and stopped dead. How many of today's big hitters among the tournament professionals could do that? Few indeed.

Then Bruen suffered a disaster. He was moving a piano for some friends and as someone let go the weight of it came to him and it tore the ligaments in the back of his right hand. He competed after his accident still, and even played in championships, but he was never quite the same player. The hand is a most complicated mechanism and, although the very capable Irish surgeons did their best to help him, that hand was always a weak link in his game. I used to play quite a lot of golf with him, right until he died just a few years ago, aged fifty-one, leaving a marvellous family and a fine insurance business in Cork, which he built up from scratch himself. A heart attack cut short his full life, but how he smoked! He lit 'one fag from another' with his strong nicotine-stained fingers. His heart went a few days after a golfing visit to Penina where he had a flat in the grounds, which his widow Nell still uses.

Sandwich 1934

I have a special affection for this picture, taken near the first tee at Sandwich in 1934 after I had opened with scores of 67 and 65, which is still a record for the first two rounds of any major Open. I was talking to old J. H. Taylor (nearest to me), Jimmy Braid (in the middle), and Ted Ray. They were three of my golfing heroes and here was I on the brink of making history – the first home player, I hoped, to collect the big gold medal since 1923.

I am proud to say that although I was only twenty-seven I had played quite regularly with these great masters. We liked one another and I think they appreciated my enthusiasm and ability. They were founders of the P.G.A. and I was a newcomer, an ex-college boy turned professional, the first outsider, as it were, in British professional golf. At the age of sixteen I became an assistant to George Oke at Fulwell Golf Club, qualified as a member of the P.G.A. two years later, and have been a member ever since.

After the prize-giving at Sandwich I took the cup to the now defunct Guildford Hotel, right on the sea front, to show it to Harry Vardon who had come to Sandwich to see the play but was taken ill and had to stay in bed. I went to Harry's room and gave him the cup to hold again. He had won it six times, and with the trophy in his arms, tears began to run down his face. I sobbed unashamedly too! A moment to remember.

There should be no bad players if the claims of one golf club maker were really true. 'Our clubs have built-in corrective action so the hands and club heads are synchronized and go through the impact simultaneously.' If you believe that, the sky's the limit, etc.

If you don't have a very free left ankle joint you can let your left foot slew round with the left hip. This is a good safety slide to take the danger off the left hip joint and spine.

Harry Vardon always claimed the upward or backswing is everything. If this part of the action is correct, correct for a particular player, then little attention need be paid to the downswing even though it is really the effective part of the stroke.

Is it necessary to stalk all over a green to find the line of a putt, or is it enough to take one look from behind the ball? Many champions think that too much searching can be confusing, so try to find the line quicker and see what happens.

A slightly open stance is not old fashioned at all and can help golfers to get the ball to the left of the target despite the fact that it is a recognized slicers' stance.

In his heyday Alexander Stanley Herd, although only 5ft 9in. tall, had almost the widest stance at address, the width to the outside of his feet very nearly three feet. Have you ever tried this, or even measured your stance width?

Another Runner-up

Doug Sanders has what is probably the widest money-making stance in the modern game and with it went the shortest backswing in top class golf. The joke they made about his swing was that 'he could play from inside a telephone box'! All the same, he hit the ball with a tremendous flail, and a long way. When you see a wide stance working you realize it does cut down a lot of the fancy hip and body work seen in the more classical swings. Doug was a very fine player in his best days, a wonderful improviser of shots who had always used a stance 'wider than his shoulders'.

He has made big money out of golf, but wear and tear of living life to the full caused him to concentrate more on business and get out of 'marking a card' for a living. His greatest golfing tragedy came on the famous old 18th green at St Andrews. Four to win in The Open in 1970! A bold second which finished eight yards past the flag, a first downhill putt, which finished four and a half feet short of the flag, leaving him the hardest putt in the game, downhill with a left-to-right borrow. *This* for The Open! Every pro's dream! There it was, one stroke off fame and fortune! Alas, he nervously pushed it straight at the hole and it faded away to the right, on the 'sucker side' as the pros say. A tie with Jack Nicklaus, only to lose on the play-off by a shot! Runners-up don't count – there is one (at least) every year. Who recalls them?

How long does it take an average player to learn to play golf, starting as a beginner? Some have real talent and can achieve a good standard more quickly, but to play only occasionally, and then to learn the rules and etiquette as well, I reckon takes about three years.

Avoid any temptation to practise too much just before a golf tournament. You should know your game already. The hours before the tee-off are for warming up, getting the feel of the club in your hands, and for small adjustments – not risky experiments. Players have won major tournaments, and made golfing history, on days when they have been unhappy with their game. On those days the need is simply to stay calm, take no chances, and play the strict percentage game all the way round.

Could you, if called upon to do so, hit a pitch and run shot twenty yards, thirty yards, perhaps forty yards by feel alone? Or must you judge the shot with eye and hand combined? It is invaluable practice to learn the feel of a fixed-distance pitch, and the sound made at impact. And the player today has the disadvantage of a ball that really does 'speak' when struck.

The golf swing is not a simple to and fro motion as though the club head was sliding along a track. The head of the club loops at the top so that the swing becomes continuous. There is no stopping and reversing direction as there would be on a track. This loop was first noticed when slow-motion film techniques were developed and Bobby Jones demon-strated for the cameras with a light fixed to the head of his club.

Roberto de Vicenzo

I was at the back of a crowd eight to ten deep behind the 11th green at Wentworth when Gary Player was playing Jack Nicklaus in a Piccadilly World Matchplay final. Nicklaus had put his ball about five yards above the hole and Player had pitched one which landed just beyond the face of the upslope; back-spin brought the ball back and it ran down the slope and unluckily finished about ten yards from the flag, when it had actually pitched only three yards from the hole.

Two golfers in front of me were discussing the play and one said, 'That is what I always want to do: bring the ball back just as Player has done there.' I leaned forward and said, 'Excuse me, Sir, but what is your handicap?' Not recognizing me he replied, '14'. So I said, 'Excuse me again, but you don't want the ball to come back: you want it to go forward.' I disappeared quickly!

The strong Argentine professional Roberto de Vicenzo has made international golf history, and a name as Argentina's greatest sporting ambassador, for over thirty years. A most consistent striker of the ball and so sweet-swinging and powerful. He's the one man whose swing might even be considered more elegant than that of Sam Snead.

Here he is with his controlled backswing and 'picture-frame' finish – an anti-hook action. Always on balance. He never needs to force a shot. I didn't think he was a bad putter at all though he always said his putting was not good. He missed a few, naturally, but you can't win 130 events and be a bad putter!

My Hero

With Jack Hobbs

Alleyn's School under-14 cricket team, 1920

The object of the swing is to find the back of the ball with the centre of the club face – cleanly, squarely and consistently. It all sounds simple, but it means that you can move away from the ball on the back-swing and move with the ball on the follow-through. Just let yourself go. The shaft after all is just an extension of your arm and the club face should be in line with your right palm at impact if you use a classical grip.

Harry Vardon, a fabulous pitcher of the ball from eighty yards in, always advised a full wrist cock for short shots, and even a full pivot. This helps with the direction, timing and narrowing of the arc. But Vardon had no problem in narrowing his own arc : the bending of his left arm narrowed the swing quite enough. Today, more golfers are giving the bent left arm a try for it certainly does relieve a lot of tension in the backswing.

Nothing pleased me more as a schoolboy than to watch that master cricketer Jack Hobbs batting. I used to sit inside the ropes at The Oval, home of the Surrey County Cricket Club, having come up from East Dulwich, London, on a twopenny day return tram ticket. I would buy a programme, mark the scores, keep the bowling averages, do everything but play in the game, and I dreamed that I would be in a star role one day out there. I played for my under-14 school team, seen here in 1920. I am in the centre, front-row; the scorer is wearing his cadet corps uniform.

My brother and I used to spend as many days as we could during the school holidays watching Surrey when at home, and I was fascinated by the way Jack always had so much time to play the ball. It didn't matter how fast they bowled at him, he never hurried, and never needed to duck. He said that his bat was quite enough protection and I suppose if you'd asked him about protective headgear, he would have said that he didn't think it necessary. In those days they didn't think about getting hit. Maybe the bowling wasn't so fast, though I can't believe that; there were powerful players in England and Australia, always, who could sling it down pretty well.

Jack played a bit of golf and ran a very successful sports shop in Fleet Street, London, for many years. He had his own special way of educating his hands to move fast. He would place a penny on the back of his hand, clench his fist to make the coin jump, and then catch the coin before it started to fall to the ground. It needs fast reactions to do that. Everybody has a training secret. Sir Jack Hobbs, as he later became, was a great credit to his profession, a real gentleman in the days when the pros walked from the pavilion by a different gate from that of the Gentlemen. The social order was very like that in golf in my early days when golf pros were not allowed in clubhouses anywhere.

I was responsible for forging a link between the Oval and the P.G.A., as our tournament offices are in a part of the premises of this famous old cricket club in South London.

Archie Compston

Archie Compston was one of the great, unforgettable characters of golf between the wars; a massive hail-fellow-well-met type who would slap you on the back in greeting and make your teeth rattle because he didn't appreciate his own immense strength. And how he loved a bet. The bigger the risk the more he seemed to enjoy it. It was Archie, of course, who played the famous seventy-two holes match at Moor Park (in Rickmansworth, Hertfordshire) against Walter Hagen and gave him an awful beating. Poor Walter walked right into that one. He stepped off the ship from New York and met Archie on the first tee the very next day, having had no time to regain his 'land legs' after a week at sea. To the amazement of many, and of course to the delight of Archie, Walter lost by 18 and 17. In fact, it was no match at all, but Hagen very sportingly agreed to finish the game as they only played one hole on the second afternoon.

Archie was pro at Coombe Hill Golf Club, Kingston, Surrey, for some years and one of his great pleasures was to 'insult' nicely all and sundry. He would stand on the first tee at Coombe Hill at the weekends asking, 'What do you think you can shoot?' (a phrase he acquired from his American visits). The fellow might say, 'Well, Mr Compston, I am 12 handicap,' to which Archie would reply, 'You're never 12 handicap! Tell you what I'll do, I'll bet you £5 a stroke on 18 over par, 19 over, 20 over, up to 25 over the par score.' A real insult. In effect, Compston was saying, 'You can't break 90 and you'll be pushed to score anything better than 97.' So Archie would provoke him to get his bets on, knowing this fellow wouldn't bet anything like a fiver a shot normally – £1 perhaps on the round at the most. He would make a book, and on a Sunday morning he would get dozens of these bets going. Then he'd go out to the 8th hole nearest to the clubhouse, see how they were doing, and accordingly make more bets. He would bet another member, for example, that he couldn't come back in 45! It became quite a profitable gaming business. He made so much money at it that questions were asked about Income Tax liability and I think it even went to the House of Lords because he made a colossal sum annually on bets which in those days were not taxable.

The last *Daily Mail* Tournament before the war was the usual 72-hole affair and Archie and I tied and had a 36-hole play-off for the £350 first prize. As a rule on these occasions the senior player usually proposed that the finalists share the total prize money for first and second place. After all, we were professionals; it was a week's work for us. It would make a big difference, after having played six rounds, to find that the game hung on one shot which could mean a difference of perhaps £150, worth at least £1,500 today. I was quite prepared to share with Archie, but when I went into the locker room I heard him say to one of his friends, 'He's not used to playing for money so I don't think I'll split.' So I said to myself, 'No, you bloody well won't split!' That, of course, was more than enough to inspire me. I beat him. But he was a very good sport and we were always good friends.

Archie was one of the first to start breaking

down the barriers against pros using the clubhouse and he was always very familiar with people, perhaps too familiar at times. Many people rather resented it. He got this habit from playing in America so often. He rather liked the American atmosphere and style, and used to wear two-tone shoes and sports shirts with no tie, which was really quite unconventional in those days.

Archie was always a very good putter. He used to put a lot for money and I think that's very good practice. There is a beautiful putting green just outside the clubhouse at Coombe Hill and he found it was one of the best ways of tuning up to bet on yourself. It is not a question of how much you might win; more a question of your own pride in not wishing to lose. In my playing days we used to chip nearest the flag in the evenings when we had already played thirty-six holes of golf. There were a lot of good scratch amateurs close to me in pre-war days, and we used to go out at Ashridge, or wherever I was pro at the time, in the evenings after thirty-six holes of golf and chip for an hour or two around a green playing 'nearest the pin, half a crown each in the pot'. The fellow who won picked the next spot to play from, so naturally if he thought you couldn't play a loose soft pitch, for example, he would take you to a spot where it was demanded. It was a marvellous training. Either you learned to play all the shots or you were constantly paying up. It is a lesson many young players could heed – 'pay or play'. Hitting bags of golf balls in a field in aimless practice is of little use. It lacks the competitive edge which sharpens the concentration.

> A useful tip for playing into the wind is to shorten your grip on the shaft. It helps to hit the ball thinner, and a half hit ball produces the ideal flight into the wind.
>
> If a four-knuckle left-hand grip is a hooker's grip, why are there more slicers than hookers in the game? I suppose because it is an easy grip to take and it feels strong. But the truth is that with a four-knuckle grip the left hand either blocks the face open or, if you release the hit early, it smothers the shot. A four-knuckle grip can be a success *only* if it is used for pushing the ball and not for whipping it.

A Power Man

One of golf's most cruel tragedies was the early death of Harry Weetman who was killed in a car crash; he was a front-seat passenger in his own Rolls-Royce, driven by a friend. Harry was renowned as a long hitter, and when you look at those long muscular arms it is hardly surprising. He stayed well behind the ball and hit past himself. He never leaned into the ball at all, but hit like a boxer, bracing the left leg and punching against it.

Harry developed his arm muscles by chopping trees as a money-earning hobby when young and that remained his favourite training exercise. Despite staying behind the ball, he was never able to stay on an inside to out arc; he power-faded or even sliced every stroke. Apart from his great power, which reduced most courses to a drive and an iron shot, he had a delicate short game and was a very good putter. Really, his wins came on the green, not off the tee shots.

Transport

When I first became a full professional I was living in East Dulwich, but my first pro job was at Langley Park Golf Club, Beckenham, Kent, which was quite a cross-country journey. I took a No. 37 bus to Herne Hill Junction, then a train from there to Beckenham Junction, and from there my old Raleigh three-speed bicycle, which had carrier, a heavy chain guard and an enormous acetylene headlamp. Often with golf clubs on my back and my zip bag with golf shoes and sweaters too, I cycled the four miles between Langley Park Golf Club and the railway station most days of the year. So, as you can imagine, at the end of a few years, before I owned a car, my legs got pretty strong. Since those days I have owned all sorts of motor transport, including a Rolls and even an old James motorcycle during the war years.

It is right to look directly at the point of the ball where you intend to strike it rather than to take a general vague look at it.

An analyst has claimed that sixty-eight per cent of the shots played are *not* full shots. Some forty-three per cent are putts and twenty-five per cent are pitches, chips and sand shots. These figures are worth a little thought. Small wonder that some pros spend up to three hours a day on their short game.

I rather like American author Dick Aultman's quip about the beginner who decides that he is, 'Going to move heaven and earth' to master the game. He usually starts with the latter!

A certain cure for the 'twitch' on the greens would probably bring fame and fortune to the inventor – and the undying gratitude of countless thousands of golfers throughout the world. There is no magic cure but here is a tip that does work for many players. Let the putter shaft ride on the top of the right hand, rather like using a pencil; it certainly helps to stop that fatal jerk.

Swinging without a ball is like shadow boxing in a gym. There is no impact. Hitting a rubber tyre regularly is comparable with using a punch-bag: it is a muscle-builder.

A hankerchief or club head cover placed under the right armpit and held there will often cure a shank.

Man v. Machine

This is a very simple, almost hand-made putting machine. It worked on the dropping weight principle. There is a small calibrated strip in which you could put a stop, then you pulled the head of the putter back like a hammer to certain scaled points and let it go, and it would hit the ball fixed distances as the blow was always the same. I thought this is it, now I have got to try and find out how to learn to swing a putter like this machine. But I found that even with this machine I would still back the top human putters, Locke especially, to beat it. Because by the time you had placed it, aimed it, tried to adjust it for the drag of the grass, tried to check the slopes, and everything else, it was still not a certainty that you were going to hole the putt. I realized after all that you *could not* putt mechanically. The best thing to do was to get a good stroke and try and aim your stroke as it were on the line and rely on your feel or touch, because every putt is a straight putt in the end, as it is with this machine. You just have to judge the grass and the slopes. I wasted years finding out there is no stroke that will last a lifetime, alas! You are naturally a good putter or you struggle to be one; to *master* this 'simple' part of

the game of rolling a golf ball along the ground is not given to everyone! To do this part of the game successfully, which after all requires no strength, is not as easy as it looks, for a sort of computer-type brain is needed in order to see everything *before* the putt is made and not after, when it is too late and the putt has been missed. As I heard in my youth when I tried a missed putt over again, 'Any fool can do it a second time' just as one can be 'wise after the event'!

Course Making

When I am asked to go and look at a piece of ground suitable for a golf course this is the plan scale (1–2000) from which I like to operate. Here is wonderful ground for any golf course architect. As you can see, this fabulous area in the centre of France is quite wooded, so it is a question of clearing the ground rather than of planting trees, which is entirely the reverse of the situation that was presented to me at my home course at Penina. There I started work on a flooded rice field without a tree and ended up with a forest, planting 360,000 seedling trees in the process, which in twelve years were up to eighty feet tall.

Bob Charles, Sevvy and Percentage Play

It is somewhat unfair to pick on left-hander Bob Charles in trouble because he was, and certainly still is, one of the straightest golfers of the last two decades. Here he is on his way to winning the 1963 Open at Royal Lytham and St Anne's and he is in lots of trouble. Bob, a New Zealander, is a bit back from the face of the bunker here and he has played the ball out with wooden wrists which is a very good way to escape from sand if the ball is lying well and you want distance.

There are players who, because of their erratic driving, become superb recovery players. I suppose the one that comes to mind first of all is Arnold Palmer and now, in the same mould, there is Severiano Ballesteros who won The Open at Lytham on the same course as Charles did sixteen years later with great recovery play. Sevvy gives the ball an enormous thump, walks rapidly after it, and thumps it again out of whatever jungle he gets into – and with surprising success. He has played incredible recovery shots from the most frightening places at Birkdale, Turnberry, St Andrews, and Royal Lytham. But St Andrews was perhaps his biggest problem, because certain holes there demanded extra thinking. The out-of-bounds danger is a constant menace on the way home on the 'old course' and sure enough he fell for it, which is, I suppose, the reason why he did not finish well in the 1978 Open. But the next year, 1979, he was all over the place and yet won splendidly.

The most important thing about recovery play is to know what is on and what is not. You must play the percentage shot, or must you? Sevvy always has a go. Too many players are ambitious beyond their capabilities; they take a club which has not enough loft, or they attempt to go between two traps which are dangerously placed, attempting to play a superstar shot which requires more accuracy than they can achieve. They just will not accept the minimum penalty and often end up taking a lot of punishment by gambling against the odds.

Here is Sevvy Ballesteros: the short pitch with the full pivot, club face fully open; a super position.

Above: Bob Charles Right: Sevvy Ballesteros

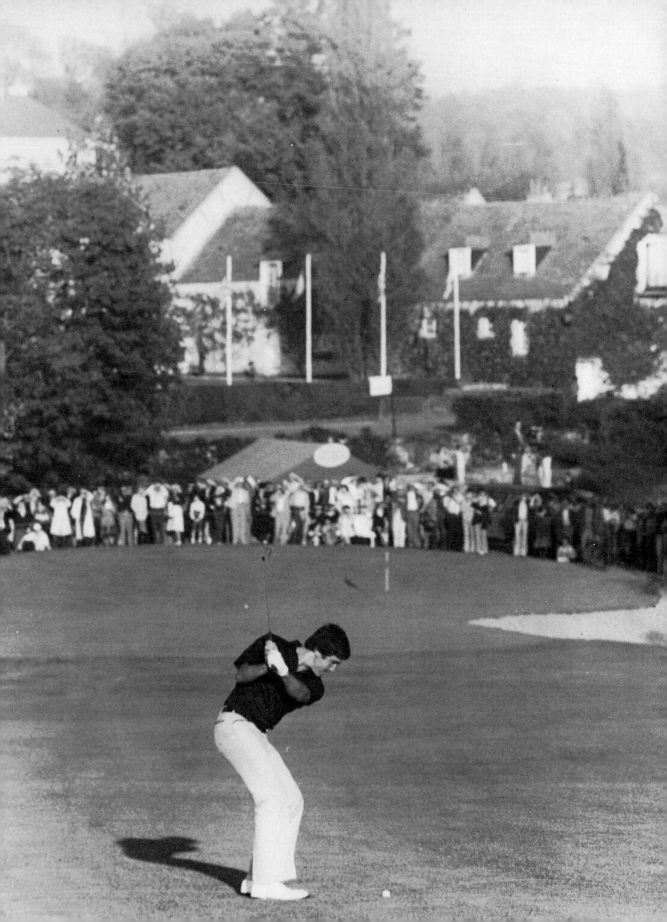

Inventions

Quite a selection of curious clubs, from the Royal and Ancient Golf Club of St Andrews' museum in the old clubhouse. On the left is one of the original centre-shafted putters, with a hickory shaft of course. There are very few of those about today. Then there is a bunker club. The idea of this design was that the sand would spurt through the hole as the shot was played and so create less resistance to the smooth passage of the club head. Next is the work of an inventor who added an angled mirror to the club head so that he could see both ball and hole when putting. And finally there is a hammer-headed putter which is really an excellent idea but alas is ruled illegal because the width of the face is less than the depth of the club. Many of the 'latest and greatest' golf club design inventions are to be found in this museum at St Andrews.

Bobby Jones once said, 'If ever I needed an eight-foot putt, and everything I owned depended on it, I would want Arnold Palmer to putt for me.' This certainly was true some twelve or more years ago, but now Arnie has some trouble with his holing out. It is not his method, nor a lack of concentration. It is simply the years catching up. But as competitive golf is still Arnie's life, he goes on testing himself against youth. Will golf as a senior offer him a new career?

Despite what you read it is *not* essential to 'freeze' the last three fingers of the left hand on the shaft. Some golfers need a slight loosening of these fingers, making the real grip with the index finger and thumb.

A painful 'tennis elbow' condition of the left arm can result from using a four-knuckle grip and trying to add a fast right-hand with a whip action in it. Push and whip cannot be mixed.

Robert T. Jones Jnr

I have always made a distinction between keeping the head locked still and keeping the body still, and that applies, of course, throughout the game. In the two photographs of Bobby Jones putting – he was one of the great putters of all time – he is using his old 'Calamity Jane', the pet name he gave his wooden shafted wry neck blade putter, which had a certain amount of loft. The shaft eventually split and was thereafter held together with glue and a piece of whipping. He won most of his major Opens with this repaired shaft, and when copies of the club were sold, when he joined Spaldings after giving up his amateur status, they too all carried the well-known whipping.

You can see in these photographs that Bobby has his feet fairly close together, which was typical of his stance for all short shots, including putts. Here the putter blade is a little hooded and his head is set to the right, so that the parting of his hair points almost behind the ball. His right arm is rested. But as he played the stroke his own head moved through with the putter blade, and the point that I think students miss is that his right shoulder has gone forward with the shot too. Many golfers try to putt without letting their shoulders move at all, and I think that is one of their biggest mistakes, especially on long putts. Many people try to

block their bodies and so make themselves uncomfortable. So if you're having trouble getting a firm impact, don't be afraid to let that right shoulder move. It can even initiate the forward movement.

I enjoyed many hours with Bobby at the Augusta National Golf Club, which he helped to build. He designed the course with the British golf architect Dr Alistair Mackenzie. Although a medical doctor, Alistair had a great flair for this work and designed a number of fine courses. Sadly, Bobby was, at the time of this photograph, disabled. He had suffered from a pinched nerve at the top of his spine, just below the neck. He agreed to an operation to relieve the constant pain. Much less was known about the spine in those days I suppose, and there was a certain risk. Something went wrong and a major nerve was damaged, slow paralysis set in, and Bobby's career was over. He remained marvellously brave and cheerful, loved to keep in touch with golf and was devoted to his Masters Tournament. This was played annually at Augusta National and ranked as one of the top four major events in the world of golf, mainly because although it is an invitational one it is always held on the same course, so an assessment of the improvement in the winning total since its creation in 1934 can be made.

Nick Faldo

A powerful young home pro who is making his name in golf although still in his early twenties. He is on the very tall side for golf and like the other tall 'masters' Andy North, Brian Barnes, Andy Bean, Lon Hinkle, James Braid, Ray Floyd, Hubert Green, Bruce Lietzke, Johnny Miller, Archie Compston, J. C. Snead, Ed Sneed and Tom Weiskopf – all well over six feet – he has had and is going to have balance problems. The slide with the knees to narrow down the hitting arc has to be studied and used.

Very tall people naturally have problems building up their leg muscles – come to think of it you never see a tall weight lifter. But Faldo's putting is sound and can be hot; altogether a great prospect and already well off from his few years as a pro.

I greatly admire Nick Faldo's golf but I do not think his leg action is firm enough coming through the ball – there is a general slackness in this part of his swing. It seems to show up in this particular iron shot and it looks as if his stance

Sevvy Down the Grip

Look how this young genius has handled a difficult lie. The club is held at the very bottom of the grip and he has played from a straight right leg, called for by the slope of the ground. By the way he and the crowd are following the ball he must have got it well airborne. No attempt to force a follow-through here – the hands and arms have done it all naturally. It is more than likely he has never met this lie before, but he plays as if he has been in the game for a decade or two.

At Lytham, where he scored his greatest triumph so far, winning the 1979 Open, he virtually lived in the rough, but miraculously he found the ball playable time and time again, the back of the ball exposed just enough to receive the club face. He got pars and birdies galore in a cavalier manner that thrilled the crowds as he won his first major championship.

is too narrow altogether. No doubt he has tried more width, but if not, it might be an idea.

Look at Ben Hogan's finish by comparison. Left side braced, right shoulder right through and riding high, like that of most great players. No forced 'duck under' once impact is completed. What authority. But note how the shaft has finished well down in the 'V' of right thumb and index finger at the end of this swing.

Isao Aoki

Looking at this finish of a No. 3 iron shot by the talented world class Japanese pro Isao Aoki, who would guess this, for at the address he looks like a high-handicap self-taught club golfer? He addresses the ball with his body bent over and his hand hanging down almost to knee level with his right arm straight. But once he gets started back it all seems to become a normal action and the hit through the ball is solid and correct. He has a flat backswing and a high roll of the right shoulder through impact, which might confuse some students, but the point to remember is that his powerful forearms whip the club head

through fast and square with superb consistency.

Here too is that excellent loose right leg (seen also in the play of Neil Coles) with the left toe well turned in.

The putter nose in the air is the key point of Aoki's successful putting. The ball is struck 'on the shaft' with this type of centre-shafted club. He holds his right arm straight and keeps his hands moving forward with the club head for a neat, positive action which more often than not sends the ball straight and true to the bottom of the hole. He is considered one of the world's greatest players from sixty yards from the flag.

No Feet!

Douglas Bader, now Sir Douglas, was one of the heroes of the Battle of Britain, and as everyone knows, has what he calls two tin legs – 'Never get my feet wet, old boy.' having a much shorter circuit for his blood stream he doesn't feel the cold. Here we were going to have a game of golf at The Berkshire, one of those famous courses in the Ascot area. I am wearing a waterproof jacket on top of a woollie (and probably a woollen under-vest too) and there stands Douglas in his shirt sleeves!

The amusing thing was that when we changed our shoes in the locker room together I would be picking my shoes out from under the bench and putting them on at ground level while Douglas, with the remains of his strong leg muscles, would sit on the bench, flip his legs in the air in turn, and change his shoes at eye level. It was much easier for him than bending down.

He used to play very well and the only problem was that he couldn't walk up a steep hill – you had to pull or push him because he had no power in his lower legs and ankles. He is a great personality with a marvellous sense of humour, still giving a lot of joy to people and living every minute of his life.

What They Tell Us!

We are asked to believe, and I quote:

This unique new shaft is a total re-engineering of the shaft with a flex-point some 15cm higher. It propels the club head smoothly into a narrower, more uniform arc. Instead of turning through a wide range of angles as you approach impact, the club head begins to square up the hit earlier – and stays square longer.

Your attacking plane to the ball is therefore under tight control. The low handicap player can work the ball. The average player gets a better shot and straighter shots!

(a) Radial deflection of the conventional shaft inhibits control to, and through, the shot.

(b) Stability of this shaft allows the club head to remain in the proper position for control to, through, the shot.

Enough! dear copy-writer. You are clearly pushing an 'illegal' shaft on to the public, for this would make golfing in the future far too easy. But good luck. You really worked on that script and we are all blinded by science! Or are we?

There is no doubt that the face of an iron club, from the No. 1 iron to the No. 4, will easily 'knock open'. It is not easy to square up a fast-moving straight-faced iron club anyway, but on impact it will knock open readily. Some flexible shafts will even allow torsion to add to the problem, but this can be accommodated by a pre-impact correction by the player. Top class players anticipate the knock open. Neil Coles even hoods the club face, and addresses the ball with the heel of the club in an alarming way! Yet he hits the ball beautifully. This shot shows him with the face of his club already squaring up.

You Just Make Up a Shot!

These three full shot finishes by Arnold Palmer show how this all-time great sees golf. He plays every shot on inspiration. Method is of secondary importance and I always feel I can read from these finishes what sort of flight he had in mind when he addressed the ball.

If you did not look at anything but the player's feet in the photograph with Tony Jacklin standing on the left as his partner you would be right to say, 'How can he play with his feet all over the place?' Yet it is 50 to 1 on that the shot was a punched one, as intended, in adverse weather conditions.

In the second photograph look at the height of that follow-through – right arm still fully extended even when the hit is long over. This No. 1 iron shot was certainly not a spared one.

The third photograph can only have been taken in England. If the sign didn't confirm it, the two seated Bobbies studying the flight of the ball would put the matter beyond doubt. This Palmer finished is yet another type, much more round his body, but it is more than likely the ball went as he imagined.

Crowds everywhere always enjoyed Arnie's 'have a go' action. No two swings were ever alike; he attacked the ball all the time, and still does.

Right: Tony Jacklin (left) and Arnold Palmer

A Firm Base

Arthur Lacey was a British professional who spent many years in America. He played very successfully and hit the ball a very long way from this exceptionally wide stance. In order not to have to do a big hip shift, he played the ball from a central position. This is always worth trying and the thing in Arthur's game was that he used a wider stance than many players, even for his middle distance iron shots. He was Captain of our Ryder Cup Team in 1951.

Ken Bousfield, a light-weight Ryder Cup player with a fine playing record, used a wide stance at times.

Former Sunningdale professional (now retired) Arthur Lees, who plays with a short flat-footed swing, has a solid wide stance with little foot action, and gets round in his age regularly on this great heath and heather layout in Berkshire.

From an awkward lie this player has got himself anchored with an extra wide placing of the feet.

Sandy Herd, Open championship in 1902, played sound golf all his long life with limited foot action, a palm grip with both hands and this wide stance, and he was not afraid to look at the ball.

Arnold Palmer standing wide.

Never a Dull Moment

A Dunlop win One of my last wins was at Wentworth in 1953, and an overjoyed Toots runs onto the 90th green (five rounds) to embrace me after I had just won this marathon event by seven shots. I never knew why four rounds wasn't enough to decide who was the best player that week! I never used to throw the ball into the crowd on such occasions. I think it is a dangerous habit and usually I had already promised the ball to someone, so I am still holding it.

The other Toots! Just look at that walk. Determination and purpose! Her gallery, she claims, although playing as my partner in the Calcot Scratch Foursomes, which we won. Before play Toots had said, 'If you put me in the rough I promise I'll hit it back towards the tee. I'm not going to play from the rough. It's enough trouble carrying you round as it is!'

Few have ever played under such a threat. In the event, I did put one in the longer grass just off the fairway. It was fortunate for me that the ball was lying a bit heavy and the crowd did not quite understand what was going on, for the ball *was* directed back towards the tee.

I walked back down the fairway to the ball, took my No. 2 wood, and hit the ball to within two feet of the stick. The wifely appreciation was, 'That's the way to treat you. You haven't been trying up to now.' I do not offer this to mixed foursomes teams as a secret formula for success, but there can't be many ways of making the game much tougher! I was mad, but just suffered in silence.

You cannot stare at the ball and hold it in focus for an unlimited time, that is why golfers keep changing their focus by looking at the target and then back at the ball. It means but a few seconds of final looking and then off, the ball goes before the eyes have tired. Some players just take one look and then simultaneously take the backswing. I prefer this to lots of waggles and peeps at the target.

Boredom produces fatigue, that is why when doing beneficial short-game practice it is very difficult to concentrate for a long time, even the top pros get fed up chipping and putting for long periods. Kenny Brown is sort of an exception.

Golfers who know even a little about the game know that to hit a putt straight, the blade or face of the putter must be square at impact. Remember, some players hole out well instinctively; they have never found it difficult. Others are scared and always will be. Some thrive on putting practice while others putt worse if they practise a lot. If you do not improve when you practise a lot, forget the practice. I have known dozens of good club golfers, and some local champions, who obtained wonderful putting results because they just putted when playing on the course, never on the practice putting green or on the carpet.

Pride of Achievement

The Penina course was finished. The rice field was dried up, trees were planted, the bunkers had their fringe of rough round them and soon I was knocking a ball round the course and taking a look at it not long after it was opened. The trees have grown considerably since this photograph was taken; in fact, as people say, 'You would not recognize it'. To me it was an achievement and, I suppose, it looks as though I am proud of it from this picture and this particular pose.

Very Late!

Unless you have wrists of steel there is no way that you can get that club head to the ball when setting yourself up for such a late hit. But this is Ben Hogan. He has pulled his hands down almost to his right leg and the club head is still above his head. This is no photographic exaggeration, it is the real thing – the Hogan way. Just think – how can he get that square impact from such a position? Only with his superbly trained strong hands.

He Concentrates Better Than His Brother

Some time in the early 1920s my father took my brother Leslie and I to the Royal Mid-Surrey Golf Club where the famous J. H. Taylor, one of the 'Great Triumvirate', was the professional. My father asked Taylor if he would play with us and he agreed. So my brother and I and old 'J. H.' played eighteen holes together and I remember to this day how very impressed we were with the way he struck the ball, giving a little grunt as he seemed to knock the air out of his lungs on impact. He must have been just about fifty years old then, which of course seemed most ancient to me, but now looking back to when I was about fifty, I suppose I thought I could still play well. I was then only thirteen or fourteen and I didn't expect to see anybody of fifty play golf as well as J. H. did. He played quite splendidly and holed several marvellous putts, I recall.

After our game J. H. wrote a letter to my father, on my father's request, summing up his day with us. He wrote that I had more concentration, determination and application than my brother and that I would turn out to be the better player. Here we are in 1927, two young pros, with our father. Leslie in fact played golf very well – and was also a very good cricketer – and yet when we played tournaments together (we did win a pro-foursomes once) he always seemed to be a little more nervous than I was and so finally gave up competing. He went to South Africa after the war, became a professional there, and taught golf and played a lot. He is still enjoying his retirement in Johannesburg and playing the odd nine holes.

J. H. Taylor

Putting along a line, with the club head moving back and forth parallel to a foot-long ruler, is good theory. But many very successful putters can bring the blade square at impact without trying to force this action. Many putters hit a very definite right-hand blow at the ball and then release the right-hand grip, allowing the left to take the club away on its own after impact. This can work very well for long putts and short pitch shots, and I have seen none other than double U.S. Open champion Hale Irwin with just the left hand on the club after even a No. 5 iron shot.

Our Joyce

Joyce Wethered was slightly ahead of me in vintage, but I got to know her quite well. At one time she actually did try to make a living as a pro because amateur golf costs were getting so high, but unfortunately the world wasn't ready for a lady pro at that time despite her being a world famous player.

She could be said to have had everything. She hit the ball a long way and very sweetly, with great concealed power, and being a very strong woman she could play all the shots. She was never afraid to go down the grip to pitch the ball or run it, and in the days when amateur golf was better covered by the press than professional, Joyce drew big crowds wherever she played. Always modestly dressed, in silk blouse and cardigan or tweed jacket, she could more than hold her own against the best scratch amateurs of the day, often to their great embarrassment. She was a deceptively big woman and a keen games player, having played since her childhood days with her brother, Roger, who was also a very good all-round sportsman. They played golf together on more or less level terms. Roger tied for the 1921 Open championship, lost on the play off and was Amateur Champion in 1923.

Joyce just loved golf but then quite suddenly she decided that the strain of competition was not worth it. 'This sort of golf is ridiculous,' she said one day. 'I'm wearing myself out playing like this. Golf is only a game for me.' Then she married a very charming fellow, Sir John Heathcoat-Amory Bt, in the West Country and simply dropped out of the golf scene. She was a terrific golfer and had she continued in the game I'm sure she could have been even better.

Golfers who go 'nap' on the club shaft held tightly at impact in the hands usually end up with a pushy action at the ball. When a player whips the ball that means the left hand whips backwards as the left arm gets out of the way, so the right can operate freely.

When you are playing a fun round just have a bet, actual or imaginary, that you lose if your ball does not finish past the flag each time you are, say, within a No. 3 iron distance. You will be astounded how conceited you are about your clubbing!

I agree that a firm grip on a putter for holing out makes more of a positive stroke.

Jerry Barber, always a brainy golfer, said, 'I dominate my entire swing with my hands'; I have never ceased to believe this.

When breaking in a pair of new golf shoes, or any shoes, if the shoes rub the heel, just put a score card or any piece of stiff paper, a cigarette packet will do, between the sock and the skin inside the heel. That is the end of your blisters and pain.

Cotton-built

A view of the Sene Valley golf course above Hythe on the Kent coast, not far from Folkestone. There had been a golf course on part of this land in times past, though it did not quite extend to this particular area, but it had closed many years before. When Lord Folkestone asked me if I would construct a new course for him (as the old Folkestone Club, which was opened in 1888, was in the centre of the town and the lease had run out) it was an ideal opportunity to move the few miles to this wonderful downland setting.

The building of the new course itself cost about £20,000, which is so cheap that it is almost impossible to believe; this was but twenty years ago. Today, I suppose, on the same ground it would cost at least eight times as much. But I always enjoyed the challenge of making a golf course on a limited budget, even though the

---

If you tend to look up on your putts, pick a spot two or three inches ahead of the ball and putt over it.

Do not go for heroic carries over water or sand if the shot you are intending can only succeed with a 100 per cent blow : play the percentage shot. It is not being a coward : just intelligent.

My hands are completely callous-free although I have a club in my hands almost every day and play regularly too, plus drill on my tyre. Why? No club slip!

Where your left heel is at the top of the backswing is a personal question so don't feel you have to copy someone and keep it stuck to the ground if it cramps your action.

Harry Vardon claimed the first-class cleek player is much more of a golfer than any other ; he needs a firmer grip at impact. Don't believe that a long iron shot can be played with weak hands.

There is a belief that toes out at address helps the pivot ; then feet parallel should restrict pivot somewhat and so might help those who have a loose exaggerated turn of the body. I doubt it.

Hitting balls from a bucket non-stop at a driving range can help to improve your golf game but there's one danger : if you don't do some contra swings there's a risk of back damage because there is a tendency to hit the ball too hard and too often.

architect is the loser. It is not well finished – how can it be? This particular course turned out rather well, I felt. Some of the new holes that I created have proved a real challenge, and in fact some of them are quite celebrated already. The whole course fits into a typical downland scene, on ground which for decades had been used only for sheep grazing. Most of the ground was tufty, almost like that you can see on the left of the photograph, full of old molehills and tall tufts of grass and even natural bunkers made by the sheep. A 'flail' quickly levelled this area. Few people realize that the original bunkers on old seaside links were made by sheep seeking shelter from the wind. One animal would squeeze into a small hole for shelter and over the years it would be enlarged to the characteristic bunker shape familiar to all golfers.

There is always a drag back with the hands at the start of the backswing to encourage a better flailing in the swing. This can be helpful to recall at times when the rhythm has gone.

Too many players with limited ability play their iron shots with the ball too much in line with the left heel. They can't hit the back of the ball. Don't be afraid to have the ball in line with your right foot at times. Anyway, it does no harm to start with the ball there and move it forward a little to find out what suits you.

Any position of the ball at address is fine if it works. If you have a good line and want to lob the ball just imagine you have hands and no arms and make the club head work as if you were throwing the ball up.

A golfer by the name of Bill Viele has a putter with a shaft so long (it measures forty-eight inches) that the end of the shaft rests under his left armpit and he putts cross-handed. This, he claims, keeps his wrists out of it so he putts with his arms ; and very well too by all accounts.

All golfers want to be killers off the tee ; few mentally adjust par for the hole according to how far they can hit the ball. So, if you cannot get up in two shots at a par 4 it is really a par 5 for you and you should play it that way. Then if you one-putt it you really can feel pleased !

Don't be afraid to experiment. If you cannot find the back of the ball squarely with one swing, try another, until you find one that is comfortable and works for you.

Max!

Max Faulkner deep in concentration. Max did not always concentrate enough I felt, and one story which I always recall with amusement concerns a match he played against Dai Rees in the Matchplay Championship at Carnoustie. Max was 5 up leaving the short 8th green, whereupon he announced loudly to Rees that he was now going to play with his head! So he stood on his hands and walked on them most of the way to the next tee. Dai Rees on seeing and hearing this said, 'There is no way I can lose this match now if he is going to use his head!' And as it turned out, Dai did beat him. A few years later Max had his revenge because he beat Dai in the final of the Matchplay Championship at Ganton in 1953.

Here Max is using a classical grip of the club. At times, 'just to make the game more difficult' I often said, he would use a four-knuckle grip. He was a natural player and yet said the easy way couldn't be right, it was too easy.

'At the top of the backswing your right hand should be so facing the sky, you could carry a tray on it if you dropped the club and opened your fingers.' A Max quote.

It is safer but more brutal on the turf to hack out a huge divot when playing short shots to the flag, because it means a firmer shot. I hate taking big divots myself, I prefer to get the same result from a clean strike if I can.

See if you can play regularly with better players, even on level terms, as losing is the best way to test your skill and to improve.

When you are given a putt and are thankful, never putt it, put the ball to another spot and putt it if you think you'd like to practise a putt.

A bad-tempered golfer is a nuisance to himself and to his friends. If he only realized he's a bore to play with. So learn to enjoy golf. Never seek to blame outside influences; you alone did it.

'Golf is a fickle game,' said old Willy Park, 'and must be wooed to be won.'

I think this is a rather super quote, unfortunately it's not mine: 'Leave the experimental to the practice field, the miraculous to your opponent and the heroic to the bye.'

Ronnie Corbett

Giving help to Ronnie Corbett, that great little comedian. But he sees nothing amusing in golf! He takes it very seriously and plays a very steady game. I am actually still the professional of the Vaudeville Golfing Society and have been for many years, as I have many stage folk friends and golfing pupils and had an act on the boards for a time. Ronnie looks forward to his game of golf and works at it as well as any professional. Here he is at Penina, a comfortable height for me to help him hold his head steady! Actually, this holding of the head is not a great help. It teaches people perhaps to keep their head steady for the beginning of the backswing, but after that, for full shots, there is no advantage in blocking the head. It restricts the whole action. Many teaching pros even encourage pupils to let the head go through with the club head and with just 'see the ball hit' as their slogan. *Not* head still!

Mike Bonallack

Golf Faces

Some bite their lips, others frown, some just grunt, some clench their teeth, some grimace and some blow out their cheeks, but Mike Bonallack has a specialty – he puts his tongue out. Luckily he doesn't snap his teeth together at the same time as his tongue appears. The more difficult the stroke the more the tongue comes out. He looks to be in good health here! Nice healthy tongue!

With a grip like a vice long after the ball has gone Arnold Palmer's facial expression has not yet returned to normal since impact. Note how the left arm has got out of the way to allow the right hand to shape the shot.

Arnold Palmer

Tom Watson

Tom Watson holes a putt and yells with joy.

Bernard Gallagher

Here is Bernard Gallagher 'full out' – nostrils extended, lips pressed together. Note the facial tension and the straight left leg. Bernard is one of Britain's most consistent strikers.

St Andrews

St Andrews as it once was. The majestic old Grand Hotel still stands overlooking the home green, though today it is a university hall of residence. The old grey granite clubhouse is there with its bay window and columns and clock, and in the foreground the St Andrews fire brigade, *c.* 1870, is testing its horse-drawn equipment by pumping water from the Swilken Burn. There, too, is a local gentleman's carriage – and all this on the fairway! It seems they didn't take too much care of the course in those days.

There is the 18th green in the distance, and the first tee, and the crowd assembled on this very shabby piece of fairway to watch the fun. People on the left are standing on what looks like a roadway which must have run through the golf course down the second hole. Just as in present times, there are always enough people around doing nothing, ready to form a crowd anywhere, especially if it is to watch others working.

I am very proud to be a member of the Royal and Ancient and also to be a Freeman of the Old Course – a freedom which includes the right to hang out my washing on this ground. But so far I haven't done so. I somehow doubt the authorities would appreciate seeing my vest and briefs dangling in front of the clubhouse or on the first hole or across the Valley of Sin!

The joy in playing at St Andrews is that it rarely plays the same way on successive days and is at its best when the greens vary in softness and speed. The trend to have all the greens holding alike and at the same speed has made golf less thrilling in my opinion.

Imagine that no gate money was charged at The Opens at St Andrews even when Bobby Jones drew hordes in 1927! In fact, it was not until 1933 that a charge was made and barricades were erected. What a free show the Scots had for years.

Surprising how few golfers ever carry two putters, yet it seems logical, for one has more strokes with a putter than any other club in every round, or in fact, any two clubs together and a switch during a round might work wonders.

The average time suggested for players taking their first putt is forty seconds and for their second putt thirty seconds.

Said American journalist Jim Bishop: 'A father who has not got time to drive to the delicatessen at the street corner and get two bits of sausage for his starving kids will wait ninety minutes for his starting time at the public course and then tip the starter. This is the power of the golf game in many people's lives.'

Bruce Lietzke

'Fuzzy' Zoeller

'Fuzzy' Zoeller, 1979 U.S. Masters Champion and a cheerful player of the Tony Lema mould, loves to play but underneath the playboy image has a serious winning vein. He possesses tremendous power and here shows the normal elbow spread at the end of the follow-through.

Larry Zeigler, now beaten by Fuzzy Zoeller for last place in the alphabetic list of players, has a free follow-through and there is a resemblance in the swing to that of Billy Casper in action of the feet and the spread arm finish.

Some Modern American Power Men

Bruce Lietzke, who hits the ball a long way, has been learning how to win events and very often now he is in contention and picking up a fair share of first prizes on the U.S. circuit. The interesting point about this photograph of him is that he has forced his elbows together at the end of his drive. Many golfers have an elbow spread position when this far into the follow-through, which helps somehow to hold the club face square at impact.

Larry Zeigler

George Nicoll of Leven

When I first came into golf as a young assistant, by far the best iron heads were made by George Nicoll of Leven, in Scotland. His ancestors had had a smithy in the town in 1831 and the clubs were, and still are, like Rolls-Royces in the motor car world.

These sturdy Scots hammered the heads out of a short bar of iron, placed in the forge until red hot and then hand beaten into shape. It is rather remarkable that clubs were not made into sets until the middle twenties but were produced as individual items, with the marvellous names of cleek, mashie iron, mid-iron, jigger, niblick, and so on.

There was, of course, a putter in every bag, but until irons became popular, all clubs were made entirely of wood except for an iron cleek

with a leather face. These woods of the day had great long heads (to give the golfer more room for error) and some were lofted. Some smaller iron heads were specifically designed for playing out of the cart tracks which crossed the old course at St Andrews and, I suppose, at many other links.

George Nicoll and Co. are still making Rolls-Royce quality golf club heads. All the people in the factory, with the exception of very few female staff, play golf. They know what they are making and when I help to create a new model the staff can test it too, not only with a lot of technical knowledge but also with a player's appreciation.

Here is the staff of 1895 with George Nicoll himself, the direct descendant of the forge founder and founder of the present company, on the extreme right. His grand-daughter, Mrs Joyce

Nicoll Ovenstone, owns the firm now and carries on the business with her husband and two sons.

There is Tom Charles, still with the firm after fifty years, who can still hammer out an iron head from the bar as fast as he could years ago. The value of this today, of course, is that he can copy any head to fit in a set; if you have a damaged club from an old set that you value very much Tom Charles can still 'knock up' a perfect replacement. When the firm is about to make a new model the ideas are given to Tom who roughs out a prototype design. He can produce a prototype of a new set of clubs – the whole set, from a No. 1 iron right through to the sand iron – in a remarkably short time. He must, I suppose, be one of the few craftsmen left in the world capable of doing so.

This picture is meant to impress on people that when they get their hands down to the position of my hands, i.e. in line with the right trouser pocket, the hands go forward altogether barely twelve inches while the club moves from the position it is in now to the position marked 'A'. In other words, this is the normal action in any golf swing, the club head overtakes the hands, speeding up, bringing the face square at the same time. Then the ball leaves and the hands slow up, as it were, by the shock of impact, but the club head is made to carry on to where you can see it has covered a wide 180 degrees arc whilst the hands have moved through a very small arc.

Where Is the Fault?

When it comes to putting, people finally resolve themselves into two categories: those who believe it is their own fault when they putt poorly and stick obstinately to one club, saying to themselves 'only poor workmen complain of their tools'; and those who are ready to put the blame on the club and try others, on the grounds that 'it can't be me, it must be the club'. I understand perfectly the two categories.

It is a terrific test of fidelity to remain loyal to one putter through thick and thin; on fast, on rough, on slow greens, and when playing very often. I know from experience that a temporary change, often using something worse for a time, restores one's love for the old favourite. Some players, to whom rolling the silly little white ball along the surface of the ground has never been a problem, just take any club and use it, hardly bothering to note if the grip is thin or the lie is flat. They do not bother to practise either, which is even more exasperating. They have a natural gift to perform this tantalizing part of the game with skill and confidence.

The same goes for your grip. For example, I have used a grip of the club with the fingernail of the right thumb pressed into the top of the shaft, and with the fingernails of the two middle fingers of the right hand pressed into the underside of the grip, but with mixed results. At a certain moment I thought I had the secret, only to find it was but a passing success. Hope springs eternal.

The Walter Hagen Award 1979

Mr Hector Monro, Minister for Sport, is here presenting to me the Walter Hagen Award for 1979. Standing on the left is Dr S. Leonard Simpson, Chairman of Simpson (Piccadilly) Ltd and DAKS-Simpson Ltd, who founded and donated the award in 1961 for the first time.

The award is given every year to an individual who has made important contributions to golfing ties and friendship between Great Britain and the United States. The international panel of golf writers and golf experts decided that they would nominate two winners for 1979. Roberto de Vicenzo was the other winner.

Fighting the Wrap Round

Here Tommy Aaron, U.S.A., plays from heavy rough, and to counter the danger of the club head turning over as the long grass would readily wrap round the hosel of the club head and shut it, he has deliberately screwed the face open. Only an experienced golfer would do this as it would appear that he has to get the ball anywhere but on his left. It can be called 'blocking the ball', but this is an insurance for blocking – almost a double block! The hands have kept up with the club head, the club head has not been allowed to pass them. The right elbow hugging the stomach has guaranteed this.

Hold the head steady – but not at the expense of losing the freedom of your swing. The textbook is fine as a guide but every player should find his own most natural action.

I do not believe that the weight should be on the heels at address for every player. For some it anchors the feet too firmly and restricts any leg and foot action.

Start back with everything together – left arm, left shoulder and the club in line with the left arm. Go back smoothly with your 'tail' pushed back. Many golfers swing back too slowly to maintain a rhythm. It often helps to keep the same tempo up and down and just let the acceleration happen. Snapping at the ball puts extra strain on the hands and causes loss of control through slipping of the club in the fingers.

The Brad

Irishman Harry Bradshaw was the one and only real 'looker' at a golf ball I ever came across. He is the only successful putter (and he's been one for a very long time) who has had the confidence and the nerve to hit the ball, and hit it very accurately too, and then just listen for the rattle of the ball in the can. This is the very epitome of 'it and 'ark', as the old caddies used to say. He's done this all his life and if you want to know how difficult it is, next time out just see if you can hit a putt of any length by feel alone without even lifting your head and eyes just to have a peek!

White Knuckles!

You can bet this club head will not be allowed to twist on impact – the gloveless left hand of Ben Hogan is very strong. Look at those white knuckles, braced left side, hands kept low, and right thumb position which indicates a squeeze with this digit and the index finger at impact.

Henry Cotton

UTOGRAPH
Wood
CLUBS
37|6
EACH

It has taken many months to perfect these clubs, built to my model, but we are proud to present them as the last word in the golf club maker's art.

Henry Cotton

MADE ENTIRELY IN GREAT BRITAIN

Those Were the Days

Those certainly were the days – 1938, the most expensive Henry Cotton autographed golf clubs at 37s 6d for wooden clubs and 27s 6d for irons. I sent a set of these clubs to Buckingham Palace for King George VI himself who having seen a set fell in love with them and asked me to show them to him. His A.D.C., when arranging for the payment to be made, remarked, 'His Majesty likes them very much but feels they are a little on the expensive side.'!!

The Buffer Action

When the arms pull down fast and the ball is struck, there is a shock, a 'buffer action' as P. A. Vaile, a golf student of the Bobby Jones era, put it. The effect can be seen in the way the loose sleeve of my cardigan has been thrown towards the target with the shock of the impact. There is no way a ball can be firmly struck without absorbing an impact shock; a sloppy sweep through the ball gives very limited results.

Playing the Ball as It Lies

The good old days of the thirties. Or were they? The days of 'play the ball as it lies'. This is a winter scene at Addington, Surrey, during the famous Pro-Am Foursomes. Leaning on his putter is the late Fred Robson, then the local pro and a wonderful character. On the far left is his partner, Lister Hartley, and I have my niblick head burying into the 17th green, a short hole on the now defunct New Course.

The ball is on its way towards the hole. My partner's tee shot had plugged deep into the green and in those days the ball had to be played where it lay. So my only shot was to bury the club in behind the ball and shock it out, rather like an explosion shot from sand. I've succeeded. I've got the ball well into the air so at least I haven't fluffed it. The ball is going well forward and, I imagine, I might have given my partner a chance of a putt for a three. Needless to say, I had never practised this sort of explosion shot on a green, but judged my dig-in very well.

How leniently today's golfers are treated compared to the old days. Should your ball plug into the green nowadays, you take it out of its hole, clean it, fill up the pitch mark, and then replace the ball on a perfect lie.

This is one of many factors which make it so very difficult to compare scores of today and yesteryear. Many people don't realize that everything is going for players today. They clean the ball on the green; they fork out pitch marks; they have raked bunkers; they have soft greens; they can pick out of anywhere for one stroke; they can deem the ball unplayable whenever they choose. This has always been a rule of golf, but

from a sand bunker shot where the ball is roughed a tiny bit it was often changed there and then. However, since 1980 there has been stricter control of changing the ball when you like. Also, players today have better tested equipment; better and harder golf balls that are tested in mercury for trueness; balls that fly lower with a higher compression than ever before. To think that at one time I used to take all the golf balls that were given to me to play with out on a quiet spot on the practice ground and have the caddy pick out the longest balls because they varied so much. I would never tee off with a ball fresh out of paper; they'd all been tried to make sure that they were all right.

In spite of all these advantages today the actual scoring hasn't improved that much. That ace of golf writers, Peter Doberiener, who has always a new slant on everything, researched the U.S. Masters Tournament, which has been played on the same course since 1934. He found that for the past ten years the winning score has averaged one quarter of a stroke per round lower than for the first decade, which, as he rightly says, is hardly statistically significant.

Once a golf glove has become dry and hard it can be revived to some extent with tacky paste but should only be used for practice. It is really a false economy to use anything but a fairly new tight-fitting glove. Players today tend to take off the glove quite frequently to let it get aired and dry off. Many remove the glove while putting. Arnold Palmer started a trend of putting the glove half in his hip pocket – a convenient 'parking place' and a simple way of airing the glove while not in use.

Do not worry about the length of your backswing as long as you turn your back to the flag before starting down.

I suppose the great value of a bag of odd clubs is that there will always be two or three which feel right on any particular day.

With a perfectly matched set they are either all in – or all out.

Some pros, even quite celebrated ones, are keen supporters of the 'head-through-with-the-club-head' method. No hitting past the chin or with the eye glued to the ball for them. Jack Burke goes so far as to recommend the method in the belief that many golfers, perhaps even the majority, overdo the fixing of the head position to the detriment of their action. It's a good point and I'm inclined to agree with him.

A putting grip which can work for short putts for the nervous person – the 'twitcher'. It blocks the right hand completely making for a piston blow with the whole right arm.

A very long-shafted putter, good for practice as it saves the back.

In Action Aged 72!

Penina, 1979

What professional sportsman over seventy can still produce strokes to delight his public as they did in his youth? Just one – Henry Cotton!
MARK WILSON

The Four Rules of Life for a Champion

Since 1960 one of the greatest and most rewarding pleasures of my life has been to select the 'Rookie of the Year' and encourage him with an award. Tony Jacklin, Bernard Gallagher, and Sandy Lyle are but three who have shown their 'appreciation' of the award by going on to achieve great things. To all of my star Rookies I have given what I consider to be the four Rules of Life for any champion. I think every young golfer would help his career by heeding the advice offered:

1. Live for something other than yourself. If you only think of yourself you will find thousands of reasons for being unhappy; you will never have had the treatment which you thought you deserved, and you will never have done all you wanted to do or should have done. Build up a present of which you can be proud. Whoever lives for a purpose – for his country, for others less fortunate, for his wife, for his family – forgets his own troubles and worries.

2. Act, instead of lamenting the absurdities of this world. We must try to transform our own small lot. We can't hope to change the universe, but then our objectives are smaller. To do your own job well and become a master at it is not always easy, but you will find happiness in working hard and making a success of your job, whatever it might be.

3. You must believe in the power of your own will. I do not believe that the future is completely pre-determined. Whoever has the courage and strength of will can, to a certain extent, control his destiny. Obviously, we are not all-powerful. Individual freedom has its limits, but freedom lies between the boundaries of things that are possible and our own will. We must always discipline ourselves without thinking of the limitations. Laziness and cowardice are weaknesses, work and courage are acts of will. And strength of purpose is, perhaps, the queen of virtues.

4. Never deceive. Faithfulness is perhaps as valuable as strength of purpose. It is not an easy virtue. You must be true to your promises, to your contracts, to others and to yourself.

These rules are very harsh, but you must add to them a sense of humour – it will enable you to smile at yourself, and with others.

Take a Divot!

Sir Alexander King from Glasgow was a fan of mine for many years, since long before the war in fact. He eventually owned a chain of cinemas in Scotland. Golf was his whole life, after his family and his job. Alex often used to come and play with me and I had to try and teach him to take a divot!

When I went to play at Carnoustie in the 1937 Open, the only hotel, The Bruce was full, so Alex found us a little pension which we took for a month, although we only used it for about two weeks. We filled it with friends and had a wonderful time there. On one visit to see us he brought a big piece of brown paper and a length of string 'to take the Cup back'! He had a great sense of humour. He never seemed to mind Harry Lauder's version of how he started to make his wealth – 'as a programme boy in a Gorbals theatre, who ironed old programmes and resold them'.

He worried about being unable to take a divot. He was a shortish fellow, with a fast, limited backswing, and he couldn't seem to get any club even to touch the ground. I could never get him to use his knees or get his wrist action sufficiently late to hit into the turf, and this became a joke between us. Then one day, after I had been on a golfing trip to Scotland, I opened a parcel which had arrived at my London house and inside was a huge divot pinned to a piece of cardboard. Underneath was a message: 'I took it yesterday!' Alex's humour. I thought it was fun teaching him golf, as there was always a lighter side to the game. This great human being really got the maximum out of life.

Strong Everything!

To get fit for golf you must build up your muscles. You can overdo it, of course, and lose your touch. You can lose your flexibility by excessive weight lifting, though running, skipping, and jogging are the popular exercises now.

I have done a certain amount of daily exercises all my life, much less strenuous as I have grown older, but this picture shows me touching my toes over my head, and doing it without any problems. In fact, now over seventy-three years old, I can almost do the same thing.

What I found was that by keeping my body supple and by hanging on my trapeze bar, which I do every day quite faithfully, just for a very few seconds, I keep my shoulders loose and keep my hands and wrists supple and free. In fact, considering the operations I have had recently I have done pretty well to get back to hitting the ball quite strongly. My general physical condition has helped.

When young golfers come to me for advice, I rarely find one strong enough. They do not hit the ball quite far enough to compete easily; a lot of them work on their long game hitting golf balls hard as they can; they learn to strike the ball better and increase their length, but very few become big hitters. So most of them set off with a handicap, as today with the watered courses and the added length on the holes, golf, unfortunately, has become a power game. I detest it, but it is true. I would rather have had the game with the courses narrow and fast and firm greens, so that touch is the big requirement and not power.

Championship golf should be a game for everybody, not just for a few powerful chaps. It is possible to win even if you come straight from a driving range, because you can learn to hit the ball onto a target, and once you can hit the ball with a full swing to a length with every club, if you are not given any freak shots or any shots that require experience and imagination, you are almost there, if you putt well. So it becomes a question of how near you knock your second shots with a lofted club; and if you have a putting streak, as occasionally you do, you get a new power player coming right into the picture.

The thing that I have found interesting in the last few years is watching the lady proettes play golf. I have taught a lot of girls, but after watching the best ladies I realized that unless they play on courses which are around 6,000 yards they do not show up at all alongside men.

You can repair a ball mark on the green but not always a spike mark unless it is in a competition in Europe. This rule must be changed to allow all green damage to be repaired. It is just too easy for putting surfaces to be damaged, either intentionally or quite innocently, by the early players in a round scuffing the green surface with their long studs.

Jerry Barber reckons that the present fourteen-club set favours the long hitters who have no need of more than two woods and works against the shorter players who would benefit from being able to carry four woods. How you compose your set is still optional.

Lee Trevino stands very open at address, with a wide stance, and plays very good golf. This stance was very popular during the first thirty years of this century but then went rather out of style. Perhaps it would suit many players of today; certainly many stand far too narrow and too shut.

Few golfers hook the ball badly because their swing is too much inside to out. The fault usually comes from slipping of the club and hooding of the club face. A good solution is to use a No. 3 wood until the connection can be made solidly and consistently with a straighter-faced wood.

A Close Look at Severiano Ballesteros

The high-speed camera of Bert Neale takes a close look at Sevvy Ballesteros, Open Champion of 1979 (the youngest-ever champion) and U.S. Masters Champion of 1980.

1. A solid comfortable stance, feet parallel, left toe definitely square to the line of flight. This is not unusual and doesn't look odd, though many other players would do better with the left toe in.

2. 0.42 seconds after the start back. The club head is pushed as far as possible from the body to make a wide arc, the hips resist the push. 'This is the start also of strain on the spine,' he says. 'My right arm takes the club away.'

3. 0.80 seconds. The wrists have cocked fully and the whole frame of arms and club is lifted as high as possible with the right hand almost head high. Club face quite closed. Back twisted to the human maximum, shoulders beyond, a 'face the target squarely' position.

4. 1.00 second. The arm frame untouched, just pulled down, wrists fully cocked. This narrows the arc, as the hands pull down and in towards the trouser pocket. The slide of the knees has helped in the arc. 'I count on my right side for 70 per cent of the power,' says Sevvy.

5. 1.04 seconds. The left arm begins to bend, raising the hands to avoid any chance of hitting the ground before the ball. Wrists still cocked, hands in line with the leg and the arc has narrowed by 12 inches on the way down from the position in picture 2.

6. 1.10 second. Here we see the hands go forward 12 inches and the club head move about five times the distance. The hands in this case are in the *actual* address position, but 8 inches higher up from the ground. So all the speed has occurred *before* the impact, as happens when the powerful right hand comes in and causes the widening arc. As the centrifugal pull acts, it is compensated for by the lift of the left arm and hands.

7. 1.66 seconds. What a free finish! Few men have done this swing in golf.

Sevvy has had a pain in his back since he began hitting hundreds of golf balls seriously every day from the age of twelve. By the time he was seventeen he was living with it. Doctors have claimed excessive golf has caused it, and no one knows yet if it will go away. Meantime he lives with some pain – his own observation. I suggest the only hope of a cure may be to do contras, i.e. left-handed golf swings. If there is no way to get rid of the pain, then it is a question of how long it can go on before it is too late. Sad to think of it.

The Overlock Grip

The 'overlock' grip

Due to having dislocated the first joints of the middle two fingers of my right hand in March 1979 and not getting them back to normal yet, I found that these two fingers did not grip the club as before and as I liked, and although I played well enough – almost 'did' my age in July, a 73 with a card and pencil in the Seniors Championship – I was not 100 per cent fit physically. Seeking to strengthen my hold with the right hand I was experimenting one day and landed on a grip I had never heard of before, nor had ever tried in sixty years of playing. You can imagine that in a lifetime of playing and practising I thought I had tried everything – yet this was new.

I call it the 'overlock' grip, for it is a combination of the overlap and interlock grip where the little finger of the right hand lies on the second finger of the left hand and the first finger of the left hand lies on the third finger of the right hand.

This means that the third finger (one of the damaged ones in my case) of the right hand is strengthened.

This extra fusing of the hands in the centre of the grip makes the hands act as one, and gives the right hand a better chance to act to the full without overpowering the left in any way. It works for all shots – even from the sand and on the green.

So far I am hitting the ball longer and straighter if possible – I've always driven well, the easiest part of the game I think. Here I am using it in a long-driving competition held in Britain in 1979. I hit the ball 268 yards on a dry fairway.

When I use the normal Vardon overlapping grip, still the most popular grip in the world of golf, there is always a certain movement between the skin of the front of the hands and fingers squeezing the rubber or leather of the grip itself. Not that the club shaft twists, but the softness of the flesh itself results in this for everyone. With the overlock grip, however, this movement, I note, is considerably reduced in my case. Only very few people, as we go to print, have tried this grip, on my suggestion. I have yet to hear of someone who has ever used it before. Curious isn't it?

The first shot I made with it 'worked', no pain

The ball travelled 268 yards

It is a certainty that no one, except Hogan, has hit more practice balls for longer periods of time and that no one, not even Gary Player, has experimented with more 'methods' (than Cotton)
KEN BOWDEN

It is not only the capacity to make great shots that makes a champion but also the essential quality of making very few destructive ones.

Play the shot you know you have the best chance of playing well. That is the percentage shot. Like settling at times for a good position in the middle of the green, not necessarily always going for the flag.

The fewer moving parts there are in a golf swing the greater are the chances of that swing working consistently well day after day. That is why I am doubtful of players who play on 'jelly' legs. I have always liked to see players hit against a firm left side.

or inconvenience at all, and once I got the hang of placing my hands on the club that way it became natural. I fall into it easily now. Initiates to the new grip fumble quite a bit at first (as it is so different) to get it comfortable. Several pro colleagues are giving it a trial and there will no doubt be reports on it to come. Will I always use it now? Always could be a very long time, as I love experimenting – but it is such fun being alive and loving golf.

This is a new putting grip I try often – I grip the shaft with my right hand and my extended left index finger. The right hand being 'full' seems to take some delicacy out of the very active right fingers. Worth a trial!

A new putting grip

Three Golfing Brothers of International Standing

The Whitcombe family of three brothers was full of golfing talent. The senior brother was Ernest, a delightful person, extremely good natured, and a very smart golfer. He usually held the club down the shaft, using an interlocking grip – knitting the first finger of the left hand and little finger of the right as Jack Nicklaus does today but with the left thumb 'outside'. Then he raised the club to a perfectly horizontal position and gave the ball a solid clout with his right hand. Ernest didn't worry much about the follow-through; he just hit the ball and if he followed through, he followed through! Just look at this picture of him – it couldn't be a more natural action. He could find the ball instinctively, shape it, give it any flight, dig the ball or hit it cleanly. I think if anything his nerve was a little suspect, but he played beautiful golf all his life and he enjoyed it, and I was genuinely sorry when he ceased competing. He won a few major titles but I don't think he cared much; he just loved meeting the people and playing golf.

Then there was Charles, the second of the three, and I think the best golfer of the trio, even though he never won an Open. It was said, and I agree, that he never left the centre of the fairway in the whole of his life, and this photograph shows a typical finish to a shot.

He kept his head well down always. He used to go out to play often wearing his jacket, a trilby hat and a pair of rubber-soled shoes in which he arrived at the course, and knock the ball round without ever leaving the line to the flag. He used to putt the same way, with great thick grips on his light-headed blade putter, holding the club in both palms and giving the ball a sharp knock towards the hole. He never was a fabulous putter, although he holed his share of putts like anybody else and won several major events. Here he has taken a divot. In fact, he must have had rather a bad lie because generally speaking he picked it off the top as

Ernest Whitcombe

Charles Whitcombe

clean as a whistle. The pros reckoned he was the best player anybody had ever seen on the muddy London courses in the winter. No matter how wet or muddy the lie he never got mud in his eye!

I played against him in two P.G.A. Matchplay finals, then *News of the World* sponsored events, once when I was twenty and again two years later, and lost both times. I played my heart out each time, but he simply played better. I ended up a better player than he was partly because my nerves were stronger and I don't think he enjoyed practising. He played by instinct, a 'natural'.

The youngest brother was Reggie, who was a little more powerful than the other two but had the same grip, the same idea of golf. He was the one who wrote the book *Golf's No Mystery,* and to him it wasn't. He simply said, 'Here's a golf ball and there's a stick with a grip on it, and I hold it like this, and I take it back and I just give it a whack, and I finish with a big follow-through or a short follow-through, depends how I feel.'

Seen here he is giving the ball a clip on the first tee at the Royal Mid-Surrey Club in 1947 in the Brand-Lockryn £1,500 tournament, which was big prize money in those days. This was one of a number of tournaments that I found for the P.G.A. right after the war. Reggie partnered me in 1938 in the match organized by the *News of the World* against the South Africans R. D. 'Bobby' Locke and Sid Brews over 72 holes at Walton Heath Golf Club on the Old Course, winner take all (and 'all' was £500). Challenge matches were still in fashion then. Sadly they have gone out completely now. I had picked Reggie as my partner and we won, I'm glad to say. Young Bobby Locke had just arrived in Britain. It was his first year as a pro and he was some putter. This skill never left him. I still think he was the best putter ever seen in golf in his best days.

With Charles Whitcombe

Reggie Whitcombe

Another Putting Aid – But Ruled Out

When ex-American Open champion Hubert Green's caddie crouched down behind him on the line of his putt and issued instructions on how he should line up the club face, staying there even when the ball was struck in order to adjust his machine-like man to the last second, there was an outburst querying the right of the caddie to be there. It was ruled that such a tactic could not be countenanced; it was illegal.

Hubert Green's grip and crouch can be studied here in Bert Neale's great photograph. The extended right index finger with the hands well separated is personal. It works, but for how long? It seems to me that extra fine co-ordination is required between the hands to make this grip valid for a long time.

Green also putts with the nose of the putter well clear of the ground, like Aoki. It is not an uncommon position, for I have seen this work often in the past, but the objection to putting with the right hand so close to the right knee is that the body has to be kept doubled up, making extensive practice spells painful and tiring.

Never Own Anything

Many of my friends have naturally come from meetings on a golf course. Some friendships have had extraordinary beginnings. One, in particular, started in 1956 when I had an idea that I might like to play once more in the Masters at Augusta, and the U.S. Open. I had retired from serious competition golf, but I thought it was worthwhile taking one more look at America, so I booked on one of the 'Queens' and during the preparations for the trip a letter came from the U.S.A. in which was a hundred dollar bill and a request for advice on a golfing problem or two. The letter was from somebody I had never met: Colonel J. B. Kaine of Chicago, who turned out to be a city banker, sixty-nine years old, and a golf 'nut' of the first order. I replied saying: 'I do not think I can justify your generosity by a few words in a letter, not knowing you personally, but on my way to play in the Masters I will be in New York for a couple of days. So I will contact you and see if we cannot get together at some point in my trip, where I can see you hit shots and probably help you.'

The ship was on time. I arrived at the St Regis Hotel, the bell boys had just carried up the luggage (we never travelled lightly, we had twenty pieces!) and I was dishing out dollar bills like pamphlets as tips when the telephone rang. Colonel Kaine from Chicago. We exchanged the usual greetings and then he said, 'You can't play golf anywhere if you have financial pressures; how is your dollar situation?' Well, it was still pretty bad, because dollars were difficult to get legally or illegally. 'In any case,' he said, 'where are you staying in Augusta?' I told him I had got rooms in a big pension and I gave him the name and address of the house and the telephone number.

We went down to Augusta by night train, hired a car and drove to this house and on arrival I found an Express letter for me enclosing a thousand dollars from Colonel Kaine with affectionate regards, hoping it would help me cover some of my expenses. This meant I was now in his debt to the tune of eleven hundred dollars!

The Masters finished. I did not play badly, and then I set off for the Westchester Country Club which is in Rye, New York State, having arranged with the Club's President, Vinny Ross,

for Colonel Kaine to be a guest of mine in the Club's vast hotel, where I had been magnanimously given member's privileges. I arranged to meet the Colonel at Rye Station, New York, on the electric commuter line from the big city.

It was rather like Livingstone and Stanley. We had never met but he knew me from magazine photographs. I looked up and down the platform, which was almost deserted; very few were getting off the train. Then at the far end of the train I saw a small fellow get out with a little canvas golf bag and a grip. I had not seen anybody else with a golf bag but I had been expecting a huge American-type bag. I chanced it and walked down the platform, and as soon as we got within a few yards of one another he said: 'Henry!' and I said 'Colonel!' and we shook hands. I asked: 'Where is your luggage?' He replied: 'I have no

luggage, my boy, this is all I have. Take a tip from me, never own anything. This is all I have in the world.'

I had booked the Colonel Room 807 at the club and immediately we reached the lobby he went straight 10 the head porter and handed him a hundred dollars, saying, 'Colonel Kaine, 807, look after me.' Then he marched to the telephone exchange, asked for the head girl, and told her 'I am Colonel Kaine, Room 807. When I call from the eighth floor give me a quick connection; got no time, no time left. I am a busy man,' and he gave her a hundred dollars. Next it was the turn of the fellow in charge of the elevator boys: 'Here is one hundred dollars, when I press the button on the eighth floor, come right up. I am a busy man and have no time.' And so it went on – a tour of the hotel handing out a small fortune in one hundred dollar tips to ensure good service.

The Colonel's little grip contained two bottles of Rye whisky, toilet things and a pair of bedroom slippers, nothing else. So I queried: 'Where are your clothes?' He retorted: 'I am about to fix that now!' He picked up the telephone and said: 'Put me through to the best men's outfitting shop in Rye,' and within seconds he was saying, 'Here is Colonel Kaine, Room 807, Westchester Country Club, I want . . . (and he recited a list of clothing – underpants, socks, golf shoes, belts, · suits. sweaters, shorts – he knew all the model numbers/sizes by heart). Charge it to me.' He next telephoned 'the best radio shop in town', to order a record player, two albums of Mantovani's restful music, and two television sets of a certain model and certain size. (He hated commercials and switched off the sound when they came on.) Several bottles of his favourite whisky were next on the order list, then he called the golf shop and said: 'I am here for three weeks, name Colonel Kaine.' The assistant said: 'I remember you, Sir'. He would remember him, he had just received a hundred dollars. 'I want six dozen Titlists in a ball bag, take the wrappers off,' he said. 'Always keep them clean for me and when they are showing signs of a bit of wear, change them and put some new ones in, charge Room 807.'

I thought, now what have I let myself in for? I have guaranteed him and I do not really know

who he is. So I had a few enquiries made and learned that he was a Vice-President of the First National City Bank of Chicago. It was an enormous operation and he was in charge of property and loans. He lived for golf. He lived in the Chicago Athletic Club in one room in the summer and in the Edgewater Golf Hotel, Mississippi, in the winter. He went from one address to the other and when he left, or when he arrived, he went through the same performance. He gave everything away when he left and bought a new lot on arrival; that was what he meant when he said 'Do not own anything'. So he really travelled light. I said to him: 'Colonel, what is the idea of giving all these tips before you get any service?' He replied: 'Boy, remember this, get them on the team. They will be waiting all the rest of the stay for another tip.' This rather impressed me and I have never forgotten his 'motto'.

The following morning we had arranged to meet at a quarter to nine. The bell captain rushed forward to tell me, "The Colonel is outside, he has gone for a walk, he will be back in just a few minutes.' So I waited and suddenly he appeared. He pulled a pedometer from the watch pocket in his slacks and said, 'Twelve hundred yards,' and set off down the road again for another five hundred yards. 'Now we go and practise,' he said, having done more or less his after breakfast mile.

We went to the practice ground, but as soon as I saw him hit the ball, by the sound of the balls on the club and by the different directions they took, I realized his hands were gone, and sure enough they were arthritic. Just my luck, I thought he cannot even hold the club!

The accent in my teaching is always on the hands and it was obvious that there was not much I could do for the Colonel till he could hold on. So I got an adjustable bar for him, fixed it up across the entrance to the bathroom and got him to hang on it every day, despite the excruciating pain! Gradually his hands became a little stronger, so his game improved and two weeks later he was knocking the ball quite decently. Then his stay came to an end. He was very pleased with what I had done for him and showed it with a lot more dollars. As he started giving away everything he had acquired he said,

'What would you like, Henry?' I thought to myself, I do not want radio or television sets, so I said: 'Let me have the record player and the records.' The Colonel gave away the T.V.s, all his clothes, some he had not even put on, his shoes, the lot! Then I drove him to the station and put him back on the commuter train to New York where he took the train for Chicago, with just his canvas golf bag and grip. As I was leaving he said, 'Have you got a motor car?' 'Yes,' I replied, 'I have a car in England.' He said, 'What have you got?' I told him. 'I will have a decent car sent to the docks and ship it to England to you,' he said. He sent me a Lincoln which I ran for a number of years and it was always a reminder of this extraordinary fellow and his unusual advice, full of common sense!

The Westchester Country Club was, in fact, a hotel; it had several hundred rooms and all the ancillaries; wonderful restaurants, swimming pool, two golf courses and a polo ground. I stayed on after Colonel Kaine had gone and played in the Metropolitan Area qualifying event for the U.S. Open which, incidentally, was at the Westchester. I led the field of 187 by two or three strokes with 137, and then went on to play in the U.S. Open at Rochester, New York, where I finished sixteenth, which was not, I suppose, too bad as I was forty-nine years old and had not played tournament golf for some time, and the heat was impossible!

'Are we playing how or how many?' This was attributed to Lloyd Mangrum. 'How true and how it sums it up.'

Whether your right elbow hugs the side on the backswing depends on freedom of the joint of the right shoulder and length of arms. If you cannot help getting your right arm floating away from the body, it is all right. The long drivers always do this.

How much the right hip turns back going up often depends on the width of the stance.

Many golfers finish better and stronger if they do not force their elbows together at the end of their swings.

I Like This Finish

The finish of a fairway wood, and there's no question that I swept through, hitting against my straight left side with my left foot twisting at the ankle – very unlike Harry Vardon's action.

In golf there is no one method. You play the easiest way you can. If you're not well informed you play the hard way without knowing it. I have had friends and acquaintances throughout my life who have sought to play golf the hard way. They never could see that golf is a ball game in which you can hit the ball easily while quite relaxed. I'm sure they felt you had to make it difficult, to be on the right lines.

Variety

Early in 1938 I met Charlie Tucker, the famous old star of a variety act called 'Tucker the Singing Violinist', who later became a very successful theatrical agent. He was always a keen golfer and one day we had a most enjoyable day's play together during which he suddenly asked, 'Have you ever thought of doing anything on the stage? I will put you on.' I said, 'No thanks, it wouldn't interest me very much, Charlie.' But he pressed on, 'I will give you a good dinner and we'll discuss it.'

Here is the menu of that good dinner. I kept it as a memento because, as a compliment to me, Charlie had arranged for it to be specially written with references to golf throughout. We went to the Café de Paris, that famous restaurant in the heart of London, where, as you can see, we did ourselves proud. After the meal Charlie said, 'I am going to book you for the week of 5 December at the Trocadero Cabaret.' Well, the weeks ran on and I had forgotten all about it when he telephoned to say, 'I do not think we can do an act that will be any good in a cabaret; there will be too much noise and interference.' I told him that I had forgotten about it, and that I was not really interested, but he insisted and told me he was making a definite booking for the week of 5 December at the Coliseum, with me at the top of the bill! Again the days went by and two weeks before I was due to go on he called to enquire about my preparations for the act, which I hadn't really begun.

Toots and I got busy at once – both terrified and dreading the thought that perhaps I was going to make a fool of myself. I told this to Charlie. 'Don't worry,' he said, 'if you flop you can go straight to bed and stay there for a week.' One idea we liked came from a show we had seen which featured dancing girls whose grass skirts and shoes had been sprayed with a phosphorescent paint so that they showed up brilliantly when the rest of the stage was plunged into darkness. It was very effective, so we decided to treat my shoes, golf club, the balls and my gloves to produce the same effect and from that we built up an act.

On the Saturday morning before the show opened we had a long rehearsal, complete with orchestra and all the technicians. I had to finish my words in *exactly* the same order every time,

Café de Paris Golf Club
London October 18th, 1938

Tee Off, with choice of
Caviare, Oysters, Melon or Smoked Salmon

Into a Bunker of
Lobster à l'Américaine

Use your Niblick for
Poussin Cocotte (au Beurre Tourné)

Hole out With
Marquise de Fruit Rothschild
The 19th Hole is now open until further Notice

so that the man working the lights at the side of the stage could switch the stage lights on and off precisely on cue. I found that difficult because I was good at ad libbing, but never at reciting, and that was what it felt like to me. I was not nervous of the audience because playing first class golf in front of big crowds was a bit like being on the stage. You are in front of people in a tournament, and whilst I had no ambitions really to face the footlights I realized that my role as a champion golfer was a sort of act; the public paid to see me play after all.

The act was such a success that I was kept on for the following week and although the handbills and the big theatre bills had been printed they managed to stick on a strip saying 'Henry Cotton stays on!'

As it turned out, the Coliseum was just the start. I played quite a number of weeks on the stage and often, during the summer, played in tournaments as well. One week I remember I was playing golf at Moor Park and would dash to play twice nightly at the Empire Leicester. That was crazy: I made more money that week at the theatre than playing golf! Then came the war and my curtain fell for six years.

TWICE
NIGHTLY
6,25
(DOORS OPEN 6 o'c.)
AND
9,0
MATINEES 2.30
SATURDAYS

COLISEUM
CHARING CROSS

VARIETIES

TWICE
NIGHTLY
6,25
(DOORS OPEN 6 o'c.)
AND
9,0
MATINEES 2.30
SATURDAYS

PROGRAMME CHANGED WEEKLY | WEEK OF MONDAY, DECEMBER 5th, 1938 | ALL PERFORMANCES ALIKE

HENRY COTTON
THE WORLD-FAMOUS GOLFER

CHARLES HESLOP
In the lighter side of Golf
"On the first Tee"   with
MAIDIE FIELD — REGINALD TAPLEY — TONY WILLIAMS

NELLIE WALLACE
The Quintessence of Quaintness

GEORGE DOONAN
"The Life and Soul of the Party"

NELLIE ARNAUT
& BROTHERS
In "The Birds Courtship"

FOUR LAZANDERS
Tricky Comedy Tumblers

DANNY. EDITH & ACE

THREE ABERDONIANS
Too mean to tell you what they do.

MUSIC HALL BOYS
A Burlesque of
THE GAY NINETIES

ARNAUD PEGGY
AND
READY
Variety's Funniest
Burlesque Dancers

Right-hand Slip

No matter what the result of this stroke, I think the position of Johnny Miller's right hand is not as it was at address. Something has happened. His knee action is that of an extra tall person, but his legs are strong and able to hold his powerful body in position.

What has gone wrong? Confidence missing perhaps. Either that or his hands are simply not working well enough together. At the end of 1979 his scoring was beginning to improve, and he got in contention again. Perhaps the problem *is* solved as he won through in March 1980.

A Couple of 'Big Shots'

Leonard Crawley, wearing his customary plusfours, which have been seen in all colours, together with the famous golf writer and later T.V. commentator Henry Longhurst outside the Prince's Palace in Monte Carlo. What an extraordinary pair they made on and off the course!

Some players have a 'hot' streak for a week, a month or even a full season, and it may bring fame and fortune. But the enduring players, those who go on and on, playing top class golf and winning major events, are those who know every facet of their game and are prepared to forget yesterday's gimmicks. Johnny Miller admits that his lengthy loss of form, when at his peak, probably came from a spell of wood-chopping, preparing an area of rough ground on his farm for seeding. He altered his musculature!

It is curious that today one never sees clubs that do not have a big taper on the grip of the left hand. Parallel grips, which were the rule rather than the exception in days past, seem to have vanished completely.

Always bear in mind that those very delicate little chip shots from around the green can be played with much improved touch if the hands are dropped down the shaft until they are almost level with the knees. In this position the right index finger might be touching the metal of the club shaft. A narrower and more effective arc can be produced. In fact, advancing the right forearm along with the club head, with the hands held low all the time, tightens up all short iron strokes.

The number of golfers in the world is increasing all the time and yet curiously the manufacturers claim that *less* golfing equipment is being sold. The president of a world-wide sports goods company recently told me that their current biggest-selling line was in clothes for jogging enthusiasts!

But as that inimitable English actor Robert Morley said, when asked if he took any exercise, 'Yes. I go to the funerals of friends who have been doing this jogging thing!'

One of my dislikes! Excessive watering of greens which means that nowadays the greens and bunkers are always soggy – winter and summer alike. This has to be dealt with one day; it makes the playing surfaces completely unnatural. Nature makes playing surfaces quite interesting without this degree of meddling. A course is in ideal condition when it is still green but you can sit down anywhere on the tees, fairways and greens without getting a wet seat.

On putting: Horton Smith, my U.S. contemporary was a fabulous putter in his day. He said rightly: 'Too much is done with too little thought, it must always be mind over putter!'

My Pets' Corner

I have always loved animals and I couldn't get away from them. I must have pets around me to love, and that is why I always preferred to live in a house with a garden, when I could afford to, rather than in an apartment in town.

The little lamb came into my life in an odd way. He was given by a golfing farmer to help the Red Cross at an auction. I was selling him at the end of the day and nobody bid. So I started the bidding at 50 shillings and got stuck with him. I took him home and he became a family pet until we found him up in the bedroom two or three times. Then, very reluctantly, he had to go.

We had Titch, our dachshund, in Belgium and when I came back to live in England in 1937 he had to go into quarantine. Here he is in my arms outside our house at Ashridge, which we called Shangrila, just after he'd come out of quarantine and at that moment he just hated me. He had been a good friend but after being left alone for six months in quarantine, as it was then, he was never the same dog. He was so miserable that he didn't live very long on his return to the family. I hope never to be in a situation where I have to put another dog into quarantine.

One of our poodles was called Smog because he was born in a November fog. We had him when he was very tiny and he lived to be twenty-one. Finally he had to be put down and is buried in the garden at Casa Branca in Portugal.

Taking a rabbit in hand! This is Bunny, our Angora; he was a pet too but he had to go when the war came. No food!

One of my great pets, who came into our lives by accident, was Oliver, a little brown and white mongrel. Oliver just came, he happened! He jumped into our car in the market square in Portimao. On two previous visits into the town I had given him a bun because he had been scratching in a waste bin that he had overturned. He never left us until he died, and he must have been thirteen or fourteen. Somehow he was able to look at you in such a way that you could forgive him anything. I call this picture 'His Master's Voice' – just look at that expression!

This rascal of a parrot is still with me. His name is Robert. He came from Harrods pet department and that is all I know about him. He can say a few words, knows my voice and tries to hold conversations with me. I can't spare enough time with him to make him a real pal, but to hear him make an imitation of somebody on the telephone is enough to bring the house down!

My bull terrier Johnnie was a present from Raymond Oppenheimer. He got knocked down by a car and broke his hip. Raymond took him back to his kennels to give him the wanted professional affection and he was 'repaired'. He lived in a sling and plaster for some weeks, then we took him back home again and he lived with us for ten years more, running around with a limp and sitting always 'for a slice' as Tom Webster the famous cartoonist once said. He was one of the kindest animals and when we sold Shangrila he came to live in the Dorchester Hotel with us in London. He became adored by the staff and the residents as he was so full of fun. He lost an eye when we were building the house at Ashridge; some non-thinking workers threw a stone into a heap of lime plaster on the ground and he went in to fetch it and came out with both eyes full of burning paste. Luckily I was present and able to wash them out, but one eye was badly affected. But he didn't mind, he was a real battler, full of fun and affectionate to all.

Fag was one of those irresistible little dogs one sees in pet shop windows, a lovely café au lait colour. He became one of the family when we had a house in Monte Carlo – a super dog.

My latest dog, Tommy, is a white bull terrier. he is just a puppy and learning. He is part of the same dynasty as Johnnie. Raymond Oppenheimer created the great prize-winning bull terrier strain in his Ormandy Kennels.

Here also is Pacifico on duty at Penina, just using a pause for a nibble while Eric Brown waits his turn to drive.

What Golf Is All About

I have seen them all . . . and I cannot believe that any of them, Hogan included, hit the ball better than Cotton
HENRY LONGHURST

Most people are still taught that the ideal way to play golf is to acquire a swing, to use that swing, and, once you have mastered it, it is forever. That, of course, is very wrong.

What really counts is to 'find' the ball, and that means teaching golfers to handle a golf club as if it were an extension of their arms. It need not be one specific movement; it can be any movement which will deliver the head of the golf club to the back of the ball squarely, or at the angle you choose.

It pays to study the weight, grip and length of the club you have and to build up your strength. If your club is too heavy for you – in other words, if your arms are not strong enough for your club – then you tend to use your body to add force, searching for strength to do the job that your hands and arms alone should be doing. That means players set themselves up in a certain way to try to anticipate the weakness.

I think the accent should always be put on strengthening the hands and arms through exercises – the tyre drill, finger drill, anything, so that the club feels like a conductor's baton, or a table tennis bat, so that you have complete mastery of it. If you cannot be master of your club then you are going to have problems.

Golf really is a deformatory exercise, simply because we have, at address, to have the right side relaxed and the right shoulder lower than the left because the right hand is below the left on the club shaft. There is no doubt that if you start golf, and play it seriously, as I did, from the age of fourteen, and you do not do contra exercises, you are bound to become deformed. Severiano Ballesteros needs contras in my opinion.

You have to start twisted at address. There is no other way. Even if, when you take up the game, you have a back as straight as that of a guardsman, and arms as strong as those of a weight-lifter, legs as strong as a cyclist's, you still have to get into a twisted position to hold the club and to address the ball. You cannot play with the shoulders level.

I have been asked what exercises are useful for the club golfer to avoid permanent twisting of the spine. In days gone by I used to scythe long grass with an iron club before long grass became rare. Hay was worth selling and was shaved down regularly. Then I discovered the value of hitting

a motor car tyre. That was some thirty years ago, and I still do it now.

Take a group of people – say twenty school children aged fourteen – who have never played golf before, put them in a semicircle, and then tell them and show them the principles of the game, how to swing a club. You can use the P.G.A. teaching handbook or the American P.G.A. handbook – just recite out 'position 1, position 2', and then tell them to swing the club as instructed. From the look of their swings fifteen minutes later you would think they had all received different instructions, because everything you say comes out via their own physiques – the length of their arms, the width of their shoulders, thickness of the neck, length of the neck, eyesight, all sorts of personal features dictate their movement.

If you take a group of people who have all had instruction at different places, they all have their own swings, but you find, in the main, that they have one thing in common: none of them seem to have been taught that the object is not just to do a swing, but to 'find' the ball. They hit the ball out to the right, they top it, they do all sorts of things. They then look for some fault in their swings. They say their swing is too flat or too fast, or 'I lifted my head' or 'I did not follow through', but in fact you find that the problem is that they did not guide the face of the club to the ball. I think that if people spent more time learning to do that as much as they do on swinging they would all play better right away.

When I use the word 'guide' I do not mean 'steer'. I am not talking about how the ball flies. I am talking about how you fly it, how you deliver the face of the club to the ball. The object of the game is to strike the ball with the club head square to the line you intend to fly it, and you have to have a certain amount of touch, or feel, for this to be possible.

I teach that feel is the important thing; to feel where the club face is and to bring it to the back of the ball. And if you bring it to the ball the question of follow-through, the question of steering, does not come into it at all. You cannot steer the ball. The word 'steering' implies that you are trying to do something to the ball when it is flying. You cannot steer it before you hit it or after impact.

I think the accent should be put on 'striking' from the moment you start the game, and that to project a ball there is an impact and you must realize that there is a shock coming. In other words, the ball is bounced off the club face. It is not pushed along.

When I first began to take a serious interest in golf, the great international hero was amateur Bobby Jones. Jones was then the pure amateur. In those days the amateur atmosphere was *the* one. Golf was an amateur game and pros were ex-caddies, they were not allowed in the clubhouse – that was the attitude then. The amateur was glamorous; he was the unpaid player with a wonderful free swing, a picture action, meriting the word glorious. The press stories about the Amateur Championship were equivalent to what we get today for the Open Championship.

When I studied Bobby Jones's swing I found that his hand action was particularly slack and loose. He did not deliver the club as squarely, or as solidly, as other players of slightly after his era whom I admired, like Byron Nelson, Sam Snead, and Ben Hogan. Jones's attack on the ball

was a rather loose-handed one, with a certain amount of club slip in his fingers, and he had very smooth grips on the shafts too, which would encourage the club to slip. Yet, when people asked him about it, he said that there was a buffer action in the swing. This buffer action is what we today call the impact. He was aware that there was a shock at impact. He realized that the ball was 'shocked' off the club and that he had to absorb it. He wrote about this, but I do not think that many understood what he meant. I think that what he meant was that he was hitting the ball as though he was driving it under a suspended carpet hanging on a line. The bottom side of the carpet was the height of his hands; he would hit the ball and the carpet would check his hands, and the club head would spring through below it. In other words, there was in his swing a sort of left hand against the right, a resistance to the right hand somewhere, and I think people overlooked that, and still do.

Now, when a lot of players today write on the game, they ignore it too. They have been hitting balls for so many years that they do not realize that there is a point in the swing when you have to absorb the shock, to take it in your hands. Forty years ago Jones saw this and wrote about it, and this also applies to putting. This is worth remembering.

Some modern thinking has it that the left hand continues unimpeded through impact though there is a feeling of taking the impact shock on the hands. This is why learning with the tyre, where the impact is some 200 times more fierce than that of a golf ball, you can learn to anticipate the big impact, so toning up your muscles to absorb a golf shot almost without realizing it has happened.

One interesting point. I think that golf balls are now being made harder with higher compression and a more solid feel than they used to have when I was a young player and, in consequence, there is more 'noise' from them at impact than there used to be. I am sure that I would have putted better in my playing years if the ball had given me a sharper impact noise. Now, with the harder golf balls, I putt quite beautifully, maybe partly because I am not putting for my living any more (just for fun, and so I enjoy it more), and now I can 'feel' the length of the putt by the noise of the impact – quite thrilling. 'Rubbish' you might say, but, if you want to appreciate how hearing is related to feel, you have only to stuff your ears with cotton wool to see what happens on the green. It feels as if you are putting under water!

Another aspect of feel: try wearing a thick pair of gloves. You have no feel at all for the shot. If you wore a thick glove on your right hand alone you would still have no feel because the right hand, being nearer the club head, should be the 'feel' hand, but it will be deadened. Sometimes it will help, however, to wear thick gloves when

you are putting, because without feel in the fingers you are putting with your fists and arms and not with your fingers. In other words, you are shoving the ball with your arms and shoulders.

You can have the finest swing in the world and yet not hit good shots. There is no guarantee that a super swing will produce a good shot because a super swing does not guarantee the face coming square to the ball. But you can have a bad swing and the strength to hit squarely with judgment and skill – and be a very successful golfer. Experience has taught me that the primordial thing is to teach a pupil to find the ball, without any specific swing action. Once he can make a contact he can work on a method, hoping that the method will make the contact more mechanical.

Bernard Hunt had a short backswing which he certainly would not have taught, but it was sufficient to make him a 'golden boy'. He could find the ball.

Arnold Palmer always had a rather fast swing, a personal action, tending to heave at the ball, but in that action was his fabulous gift of delivering a square hit more often than not.

Joe Carr had a frightful slashing, swaying swing, with the right thumb on the side of the shaft, and yet he was one of the best golf players in the world for a period. I feel that when he changed to play more in an accepted classical way, which he did by sheer will power and weeks of incessant practice, he was not really any more successful than he had been with his original instinctive attack on the ball. Even today, when I play with him, I still encourage him to put his right hand underneath to recapture the glory of his free, slashing days.

George Duncan, the 1920 Open champion who believed golf was an instinctive game, was a temperamental player himself. If he got a good start, a 69 was always on. If he started badly then he almost sulked. This was quite inadmissible really, he would not fight back to save a round, he just let it go to 80 or 82! Yet, he knew the game very well and loved it. His was a case of, 'Don't do as I do, do as I say.' He almost hit the ball walking to it – on the move.

What is timing? I timed that one, why can't I do this all the time? You can when you realize that timing a ball means that the left hand and the right hand harmonize perfectly. That is, the left hand does not stop the right applying its maximum power forwards while it does its maximum backhanded; only pushing when the right hand intends to push and only whipping when the right hand whips; you can't mix a push with a whip and get anywhere.

The Future of Golf – A Guess

With extra leisure days in the week surely due in the next decades I am certain more people will turn to hitting a golf ball, be it on a driving range or on a golf course, as a cheap, health-giving exercise and ideal for filling in the days.

I do not see the luxurious country club type of operation with its necessary steep subscriptions and high green fees as a golf need of the future, but public golf or even private clubs geared to a lower key are wanted. They could have bungalow type clubhouses, snack bar facilities and simple changing accommodation, so turning the clock back eighty years. Such clubs can be sited in private parks, fields or heathland, where sheep graze, the putting areas fenced in by simple electrically charged wire. Natural features like trees, ponds, hollows, etc. can be used by the golf architect to add a little interest and save money on the layout. These clubs and courses could be operated at a trifle of the cost of a big, modern course and clubhouse kept in top condition. Sheep would crop the playing areas most of the year and an occasional cut with a mower would do the rest. This would provide a place to play golf on with all the thrills of the game, but for a small annual subscription and a cheap green fee. Even watering of the greens could be an optional extra to start with. An occasional visit to play on the great courses would be the 'icing on the cake'.

Courses made with a good skeleton plan are essential and can be made for a reasonable cost still, and then as club finances permit they could be improved annually. To present a super course today, ready for play with watered greens and fairways, huge sand bunkers and big teeing areas, means spending a lot of money. At the moment courses are getting too long, it takes too much time to play a round and is therefore too tiring for the majority. All this would change overnight if a floater ball was the ball of the day.

This change to a lighter ball would bring thousands more courses automatically up to championship standards and cut down on the reign of the power players, for skill would count more than sheer strength and the day of the female Open Champion could approach. There would be some turning of male bodies in their graves at the thought of Mrs Nancy Lopez Melton's name on the old trophy plinth!

Golf equipment has become expensive like most manufactured items of sporting equipment today, so it could be that in the financial interest of the players and again to bring back the half shot into golf a set of clubs might be limited to ten, and later to seven, in the bag in official tournaments.

Golf balls could be standardized, the same ball for every competitor in the Open Championships of the world, no maker's specials! Different makes of ball could be optional in other competitions. Then we could have a standard length short spike on golf shoes too to stop the tearing of the turf on the greens – that scuffing up by clumsy walkers would be out. I would even go for moulded rubber-soled shoes only, as on bowling greens. They would be more flexible, lighter and cheaper too, and of course allow a slight twisting of the feet which would be an insurance against lower spine damage.

There could be a reduction in the number of pro events and more amateur events, which would draw smaller crowds of course, but which would make good golf entertainment on the television. Pro-Ams will continue to increase, but I do not go for the present formula where a team of one pro and three amateurs on full handicap allowance mark their own team cards!

The lady professionals will become more popular each year and I should not be surprised to see more 'Amazons' taking to golf, such as shot putters, hurdlers, javelin throwers, altogether very strong women. They will make their power count and excite the crowds.

It is a pity that many fields owned by brewers near their country inns have been sold off, because the pubs and inns would be ready-made clubhouses for par 3 courses, which could blossom and be used by beginners and even experienced golfers to form part of regional golf leagues – inter-inn competitions, home and away, 'The Bull' versus 'The Rose and Crown' for example. What a subject for a regional television sports programme, with the big-name commentators treating the matches in a light-hearted way: 'The match was lost by a nasty dandelion on the line of Bill Jones's putt!'

There will be lessons by video phone; just post your cheque, call up the pro at a fixed time and have him look at your swing on the practice ground 1,500 miles away from his phone. There might be a national handicap service. Put your identification number in the computer and your last ten scores will be given and your current handicap announced. Ideal if you've left your handicap certificate at home and it is needed.

Maybe hovercraft golf cars for golfers will come along, solar powered, and reduce damage to the turf. Pull carts assisted by solar power too.

Maybe the game is too good as it is to change, but what would a $3\frac{1}{2}$-inch diameter hole do to the game? Only trials could give an answer to this question.

Thanks for the game!
Tony Cotton

Photo Acknowledgements

All the illustrations were supplied by Henry Cotton and in the main come from his private collection. However, the author and publishers are grateful to the following for permission to reproduce the illustrations on the pages listed:

Page 9: Peter Dazeley
19: Sotogrande
21 top: *Daily Mail*
26 top: British Paramount News Photo
27 top: Popperfoto
31 left: Action Photos by H. W. Neale
31 right: Fox Photos
32: Action Photos by H. W. Neale
34–3 centre: Action Photos by H. W. Neale
37: Topical Press Agency
38: Bill Mark
39 bottom: Keystone
42 top: Action Photos by H. W. Neale
42 bottom: Photo by Frank Gardner
43 top: Photo by Frank Gardner
46 bottom: © Beaverbrook Newspapers Ltd
48 right: Society and Sports Press
49 left: Sport and General
52: Bill Mark
54 left: Action Photos by H. W. Neale
60: photo by Sidney Harris
62 top: Action Photos by H. W. Neale
62 bottom: © Beaverbrook Newspapers Ltd
65: Action Photos by H. W. Neale
66 bottom: Sport and General
67 left: Fox Photos
69: Photo-Art Commercial Studios
71: Action Photos by H. W. Neale
73–5 (8): Photos by Frank Gardner
77 (2): Action Photos by H. W. Neale
97: *Dublin Evening Mail*
81: Action Photos by H. W. Neale
87 top: Scottish Television Ltd
87 bottom: Sport and General
97 bottom: photo by G. M. Cowie
98–9 (3): Action Photos by H. W. Neale
102–3 (6): photos by Frank Gardner
104 top: Sotogrande
105: Fox Photos
106: Associated Press
110: London News Agency
114: P.A.–Reuter
115: Action Photos by H. W. Neale
116 top: photo by G. M. Gowie
117 right: Sport and General
118 left: Foto-Belarte, Lagos
118 right: Action Photos by H. W. Neale
119 (2): Action Photos by H. W. Neale
120 (2): Action Photos by H. W. Neale
123 (3): Action Photos by H. W. Neale
124 right: Fox Photos
125 top left: Fox Photos
126 top: Action Photos by H. W. Neale
126 bottom: Fox Photos
132: Action Photos by H. W. Neale
134–5 (4): Action Photos by H. W. Neale
136: photo by G. M. Cowie
137 (3): Action Photos by H. W. Neale
139 left: Peter Dazeley
140 bottom: Barry Swaebe
141 Action Photos by H. W. Neale
142 right: Action Photos by H. W. Neale
148–51 (7): Action Photos by H. W. Neale
154 left: A. H. G. Arbuthnot
155 right: Sport and General
161 top: Fox Photos
162: Action Photos by H. W. Neale
164 top: Fox Photos
164 bottom: *Daily Express*
165 top left: *News of the World*
165 bottom: Fox Photos

INDEX